AF443836

More Praise

"By any measure, Schumarry Chao's career as an Asian American woman in the healthcare industry has been a remarkable and fruitful one. Here, in this insightful and inspiring book, she relates the lessons learned from a difficult upbringing and offers practical advice on following your instincts, turning obstacles into opportunities, and embracing change in the workplace. This is necessary reading for anyone who hopes to reinvent themselves, professionally and personally, no matter what stage of life."

-Wendy Lee
Author of *Happy Family* (Booklist Top Ten Debut Novel)
and *The Art of Confidence*

"This is a deeply personal and inspirational book. Schumarry overcame cultural pressures, past hurts, and societal expectations to reinvent herself and achieve fulfilment in her personal life and in her career. With courage, insight, and honesty, Schumarry shares her real-life stories of renewal and reinvention, providing lessons for all of us in today's fast-changing world."

-Arvind Bhambri
Associate Professor of Management and Strategy, USC Marshall School of Business; prominent in global business development; *Wall Street Journal*-profiled top EMBA Professor; Mckinsey Prize winner

"Schumarry Chao's life is a vibrant example of the Hero's Journey. It fits the universal story template identified by Joseph Campbell. But she did not make it up to fit the template. She had it thrust upon her. Either she would bring a heroic story to life, or she would not survive, as the introduction to her new book makes clear. The book is worth buying just for that one chapter. I met Schumarry nearly 40 years ago. It was clear then that she would get wherever she chose to go. Her book explains how she did it and what she learned along the way. I hope she will now create a YouTube presence connected to her book. It is not enough to read the book. You need to experience the person who wrote it."

-Tim Campbell
Emeritus Professor of Finance, USC Marshall Business School; former Academic Director, Executive MBA Program; Associate Editor of the *Journal of Finance* and *Journal of Real Estate Finance and Economics*

THREADS OF A SILK PURSE

Weaving Life's Detours into a Journey
of Happiness, Success, and Prosperity

Schumarry H. Chao, MD MBA

Schumarry H. Chao
Threads of a Silk Purse: Weaving Life's Detours into a Journey of Happiness,
Success, and Prosperity

SHC Enterprises
Copyright © 2026 by Schumarry H. Chao
First edition

Softcover 979-8-9998082-6-4
Hardcover 979-8-9998082-3-3
eBook 979-8-9998082-5-7
Audiobook 979-8-9998082-4-0

Book Design | Ashley Russell Designs
Editors | Licia Morelli
Author Portrait Photographer | Cashman Pro Photo Lab
Publishing Management | TSPA The Self Publishing Agency, Inc.

*To my parents, who gave me life and the opportunity to come
to the United States.*

To my parents-in-law, who lovingly showed me the way.

*To my husband, who has been both my anchor and the
wind beneath my wings.*

Contents

Acknowledgements xiii
Introduction xv

Part One: Letting Go of the Negatives
Forgiveness and Letting Go 1
Dwelling On Things Being Unfair 5
Stop Belaboring What You Cannot Control 11
Letting Go of No-Win Situations 19
Making Decisions Out of Fear 25
Setbacks As Opportunities 29

Part Two: Embracing the Positive
Positive Company 39
Mindset and Perspective 47
Morning Meditation Ritual 49
If That Hadn't Happened 53

Part Three: Trusting Your Inner Voice
Life Changing Decisions 69
Activating Your Inner Voice 75

Part Four: Insights from Career
Opening Doors 81
Organization and Culture 83
Position and Role Inside The Organization 89
Compensation: Valuing Your Worth 95

Part Five: Insights from Career
Management 105
Managing Down 107
Managing Up 123
Managing Across 135

Part Six: The Big Picture
Values and Reputation 151
Incentives Drive Behavior. 155
Sense of Humor 159
Reinvention At Any Age 163
The Art of The Pivot 167
Having It All 175
Security and Happiness Come From Within 183

Reflections
Connecting The Dots Looking Backwards 191
Journey and The Truth 195

Biography 197

Acknowledgements

To my children, Lisa and Stephen, who encouraged me to share my story and offered invaluable guidance throughout this process.

To my surviving sisters, Joanne and Schucherry, though our paths have often diverged, I am deeply grateful that they are now coming together.

To the Tung and Tsou families, especially Uncle CK, who has always been there for us and cheered us on.

To my friends, especially Carolyn R., Lisa G., Annie D., and Johanne V., for your unwavering encouragement. Carolyn, I am especially thankful that, despite your overflowing plate, you always made room to offer your thoughtful feedback and advice.

To Licia Morelli, your editing and insight have helped bring my story to life.

To USC and UCSF, for opening your doors to a struggling immigrant and giving me a strong educational foundation.

To my employers and clients, who entrusted me with opportunities that shaped my career.

And to my colleagues throughout the years, whose collaboration, support, and example have enriched my growth and my life.

Introduction

Faith and trusting myself saved me. Long before I ever heard the word "God," I sensed a guiding force in my life. How else could I have traveled such an improbable road?

I was born a girl in Mukden, China, in the spring of 1946 after World War II. My mother, the eldest daughter of Mukden's most powerful warlord, grew up with 7 servants tending to her every need. Despite the prejudice against daughters, she earned a coveted spot in one of the first classes for women at Peking University. My father's early life could not have been more different. Orphaned at seven, he survived by selling vegetables on the street, endured constant hunger, and somehow pushed himself through medical school.

Their marriage, sparked by a chance meeting in an era of arranged unions, deserves its own book. Yet it set the stage for the twists of fate that shaped my journey.

My parents' wedding in Mukden, 1945.

When I was not yet two, my father left for the United States to pursue postgraduate surgical training. His decision became critical to our survival. In 1949, as communist forces choked off Mukden, my mother bartered her jewelry for passage to her parents' summer home in Beijing so that we would not starve. Because I was the granddaughter of a warlord and the daughter of a man who had fled to America, I was not allowed to attend any schools in Beijing. That refusal fueled my mother's determination to escape China, even at tremendous risk.

My mother with me and my younger sister, Schucherry, in Beijing.

Ironically, the very cultural bias that devalued girls opened a door for us. Officials first agreed to let my mother leave but insisted that I remain behind as "insurance." Because I was considered less valuable as a girl, they ultimately allowed me to accompany her. I was ten years old before I sat in a classroom for the first time, in Hong Kong.

Immigrating to the United States in the 1950s was virtually impossible for Chinese families; annual quotas allowed only 100 visas nationwide. Yet after just ten months in Hong Kong, our application was approved. Many others died waiting. I can explain this only as divine intervention.

Our escape was extraordinary. From Beijing, travel required direct government approval. My mother petitioned Zhou Enlai himself, the foreign minister of China, second in command to Mao Zedong, and husband of one of her former classmates. That courage saved our lives. Decades later, when China reopened, I visited our old neighborhood in Beijing and learned that only one of the fifty families on our street had survived the Cultural Revolution. Everyone else, including children, had been slaughtered.

While my mother and I navigated upheaval, my father struggled in America. He worked as an unlicensed physician at the State Hospital in North Dakota while preparing for his medical exams. The hospital superintendent, sympathetic to his situation, lobbied his golfing partner, the senator who chaired the Senate Immigration Committee, to sponsor a special bill granting us entry. Without that intervention, we might have waited in Hong Kong for years.

The year between Beijing and Jamestown, North Dakota, was a blur of dislocation. We left relatives, friends, and every material possession behind, arriving in Hong Kong with only the clothes we wore. I remember hitchhiking across the border and stumbling through a new dialect. Six months later we could speak enough Cantonese to manage daily life. Three months after that we learned our U.S. visa had been approved. One month later we stepped off a train in North Dakota during a December snowstorm, and I saw my father for the first time since I was eighteen months old.

The next morning, I went to school. That afternoon I ran home and asked my father how to say, "I don't understand." There were no English-as-a-second-language programs, so the teachers placed me in advanced math but preschool for my ABCs, the only time I ever towered over my classmates. By summer I spoke enough English to play with children my own age. Two years later my father passed his licensing exams in California, and we moved to Los Angeles.

Life there was no fairy tale. With no servants, my overwhelmed mother turned me into the family nanny for 3 baby sisters and family housekeeper. To save money, my father made me his sole office staff, handling billing, bookkeeping, and scheduling. At sixteen he tried to arrange a marriage that would elevate the family's status and finances. My mother, believing her daughters could equal any son, pushed me to be a doctor. I did my best to please them, even winning the Miss Chinatown crown, and followed the path through medical school.

Miss Chinatown on a parade float.

Becoming a doctor was survival. English remained my weak point, and my SAT and MCAT verbal scores were dismal, yet the University of Southern California and UCSF opened their doors. Although I had no calling to be a doctor, the medical education provided the platform for a management career in every corner of the health-care industry.

With my parents at my medical school graduation.

God kept placing me in the right place at the right time, each role teaching unique lessons. Growing up under communism had trained me to cling to the familiar and mistrust power. Step by step, God pushed me beyond that comfort zone. With each leap into the unknown, I gained confidence, slowly realizing that true security and happiness come from within, not from any external validation.

Over the years, I have managed health care from every angle: physician practice, hospital systems, employer benefits, insurers, pharmacy benefit management, pharmaceuticals, and academia. Because I never stayed boxed in, I developed a panoramic view of the industry that fuels creative, out-of-the-box thinking. Consulting assignments widened that lens even further, exposing me to diverse structures, incentives, and personalities. I never imagined that those experiences would one day mark me as an industry expert.

This book shares the stories of that improbable journey full of detours, not only through my career, but through my experiences with family, friends, and marriage. Each chapter represents one of the many threads that, over time, have been woven together into a kind of silk purse, a life shaped by resilience, purpose, and grace.

I hope these stories inspire you, especially emerging women leaders, to claim your own path with courage and faith. My struggles have also taught me practical strategies for surviving and thriving in male-dominated spaces. May the lessons I learned become threads in your own weaving, guiding you toward your version of happiness, prosperity, and abundance.

With hard work, faith, and a little divine timing, everything is possible. Each effort becomes another thread, strengthening the fabric of the silk purse you are creating for your own life.

Serving as Director of Emergency Trauma, Los Angeles County.

Celebrating my 70th birthday.

Our family at dinner in a Las Vegas restaurant.

Part One

Letting Go of the Negatives

1

Forgiveness and Letting Go

EVERY LIFE HOLDS MOMENTS of hurt and betrayal. Feeling anger or resentment is natural, yet clinging to those emotions blocks the positive energy that moves us toward opportunity and joy.

For years I carried deep anger toward my parents. Constant criticism, threats, and the chores of a household servant made my teenage years feel like a nightmare. I lived in fear of being thrown out, and that fear fed a lifelong insecurity.

My mother, raised as the eldest daughter of a powerful warlord, was steeped in a culture of power and revenge. After being separated by the Bamboo curtain for 8 years, my father suggested they move on with their own lives. She risked everything to come to the United States, driven less by love than ego and revenge. As her eldest daughter, I became the object of a struggle between my parents. My father, following the Chinese tradition with daughters, pushed me to marry well to elevate the family's status and wealth; my mother, with only daughters, pushed me to take on the role of son to become a doctor, showing that her daughter could surpass any son, even follow my father's footsteps to become a surgeon. Guided by faith, I found the strength to choose my own path.

Over time, I learned to see my parents' actions from a wider angle.

As the eldest daughter of the most powerful warlord in Northeast China, my mother was raised in luxury, attended to by seven personal servants. My grandfather's influence spared my father from the terrible fate that claimed so many of his friends under Japanese occupation. What was meant to be only a two-year separation while my father trained in the U.S. stretched to almost 10 years.

When Communism swept in, my mother lost not only the material wealth she had always known but also the influence and security of her family. Overnight, she was thrust into the role of head of household, responsible for her family's survival. Daily living went from luxury shopping and Beijing opera to stretching one cup of cooking oil and sugar rationed for each household per month. Her upbringing had trained her to see the world in absolutes: win or lose, friend or enemy, powerful or subservient. Living under a system where betrayal was rewarded only deepened this outlook. She feared emotional closeness, even with her children. Yet she risked everything to secure me a better life.

At the time, I didn't understand the danger when armed guards with machine guns patted me down at the border. I couldn't grasp the enormity of what it meant for my mother to cross with only her children and the clothes on her back, then beg strangers for money to reach Hong Kong. Looking back now, I can't imagine the weight she carried in that moment.

My father's story was equally marked by hardship. Orphaned as a child, he survived by selling vegetables on the street, teaching himself to read in the early morning light, and scraping by on small scholarships through medical school. He endured Japanese oppression and spent eight uncertain years shuffling between training programs in the U.S., each time finding a way to extend his visa until he finally secured a green card. These experiences shaped his stark view of the world: survival first, emotions last.

He could only see my struggles through his own hardened lens and could not recognize my desperate need for more. Separated from me in my earliest years, he never bonded with me, holding instead to the traditional belief that children were property. My independence threatened his sense of control and, I suspect, fueled his resentment. My younger sisters, born after my parents became more Westernized and financially secure, grew up in a very different household than I did.

Focusing on what my parents gave me shifted my heart. Whatever their motives, my father's presence in the United States and my mother's fierce fight on my behalf opened the door to the life I now enjoy. I am saddened that they could not share more fully in the fruits of their labor. Yet by forgiving them, I released a burden and uncovered the positive energy that drives my happiness today.

At work, I often saw how clinging to negativity and resentment could become a kind of comfort zone, with failure turning into a self-fulfilling prophecy. I recognized this most clearly with Jeff Sipsey at LA County. At first, Jeff seemed to take pleasure in undercutting me, seizing every opportunity to align others against me. But over time, I earned his trust, and we built not only a strong working relationship but also a deep friendship that lasted forty years, until his death.

Jeff was a brilliant physician, beloved by patients and support staff alike, and by any objective measure, he deserved advancement. Yet after repeated, unsuccessful attempts to help him move forward, I came to understand that his own grievances and self-sabotage stood in the way. Time and again, he made his negative predictions come true. Despite many honest conversations, it became clear that he felt most comfortable, even validated, when those predictions proved correct.

In the end, all I could do was make sure Jeff was in a stable, protected position before moving on in my own career.

We all know people who have wronged us. Dwelling on the hurt is like pressing on an open wound, it keeps the pain alive. Letting go allows that wound to heal. Talking things through can reveal misunderstandings or new perspectives. If the other person admits the wrong and seeks forgiveness, I can readily forgive. If they justify their actions, I can still release my anger, but I adjust my trust and set clear boundaries.

Practices That Help Me Release Negativity

Meditation keeps me grounded and positive. When negativity feels overwhelming, I stand under a warm shower, imagine the water washing over my head, and see every negative thought sliding down the drain. Life is too short to nourish grievances. Let them flow away, and make room for gratitude and possibility.

2

Dwelling On Things Being "Unfair"

"THAT'S NOT FAIR!" We have all felt it, and sometimes we really *are* on the short end of the stick. The trouble comes when we camp out in that feeling. Staying stuck drags us down and saps the energy we could use to move forward.

The Family Version

Sibling rivalry is a petri dish for perceived favoritism. In my childhood it was not just perceived, it was obvious. The two eldest daughters, Schucherry and me, came to the United States at ages ten and twelve and were treated like household staff. The three younger sisters, all born in America, were indulged from birth until our parents passed away.

The contrast showed up everywhere, from daily routines to major financial decisions. A few memories capture the gap with painful clarity:

- While I waited tables for $1.25 an hour to pay for school, my father offered $5,000 for a Bob's Big Boy statue because the five-year-old twins adored it.

- I earned every dollar I spent; my sisters received cars, full college tuition, even a down payment on a house.

- Family photo albums are full of pictures of my parents with the younger girls. There is not one of my parents with Schucherry and me, nor a single shot of the entire family together.

- The finale: each sister inherited a significant share of a multi-million-dollar estate, while I received a $100 check, contingent on waiving further claims. I never cashed that check.

ARLENE MU CHAO, EXECUTOR
FOR THE ESTATE OF CHING JU CHAO
1405 VIA DAVALOS
PALOS VERDES ESTATES, CA 90274-1943

109

16-7001/3220
0145091708

DATE 7-23-96

PAY TO THE ORDER OF Schumarry Chao Tsou

$-100.00

—One hundred dollars & 00/100 cents—

DOLLARS

CALIFORNIA FEDERAL BANK F.S.B.
Palos Verdes Office
608 Silver Spur Road
Palos Verdes Peninsula, California 90274

MEMO Complete & full payment of all inheritance amt. & debts of Ching Ju Chao

Arlene Mu Chao

My inheritance from my parents' estate.

My husband, Paul, and I resolved never to repeat that pattern. We focused on treating our own children equally, and the result is a warm sibling bond that has continued into adulthood.

Lisa and baby Stephen.

Halloween Raggedy Ann and Andy.

Lisa and Stephen at Dodger Stadium.

Reframing the Unfairness

Resentment could have eaten me alive. Instead, I chose gratitude for traits the hardships forced me to develop: independence, resilience, a work ethic that fueled my later success. Ironically, three sisters, cushioned by lifelong support, never launched careers or discovered their own passions. Privilege insulated them from growth.

To distance myself from the situation, I had moved out of the family home, but beyond that, there was little I could do, I had no real power to change the situation. My sense of filial responsibility lingered, making it difficult to fully move on.

Work, however, is different.

The Workplace Version

You may find yourself in a job where your contributions are undervalued or your treatment is unfair. Hoping things will magically improve is not a plan. Prolonged acceptance erodes self-worth and invites even more inequity. I watched a colleague accept the worst pay and schedule for ten years because he "wanted to be liked." When budget cuts came, he was the first out the door. When he aired the bottled-up grievances, his attorney asked, "Why did you tolerate it? Why didn't you speak up or leave?" He had no answer.

If you ever face a similar situation, here is the approach that has helped me reclaim my power:

- Gather facts. Document duties, results, and comparisons with peers.

- Address it early. Stick to evidence, not emotion, in conversations with leadership.

- Keep options open. Quietly explore other roles or organizations. Having choices restores a sense of control.

- Know when to move on. Sometimes a company recognizes your value only after you prove it elsewhere.

Staying in an unfair situation breeds bitterness; acting decisively restores power. The choice is always ours: dwell on the injustice or channel that energy into pursuing the respect and life we deserve.

3

Stop Belaboring What You Cannot Control

WHEN I LOOK BACK, I see how much energy I spent wishing things were different, worrying, or regretting. Little by little, I learned to accept reality and do the best I could with it.

THE WORRY HABIT

My mother taught me to expect the worst. Whenever something veered off plan, I lay awake worrying, imagining disaster. A sleepless night guaranteed I would start the next day convinced the sky was falling. That pattern generated only negative energy, so I worked hard to break it.

Meditation became my turning point. I began to trust that, whatever happened, it would work out, often for the best. In the beginning, I tried a structured exercise: I allowed myself thirty minutes a day to worry, then blocked out anxious thoughts the rest of the time. Breathing exercises helped me exhale the negatives and refocus on my blessings. Today I still practice mindful breathing; the timed worry sessions are no longer necessary.

THE DAMAGING NEED TO CONTROL

The emotions to control can be so strong that they drive people to act directly counter to their goals.

FAMILY

After all my mother endured, so much of it beyond her control, it is understandable that she clung fiercely to the idea of total control. She narrowed her world to her immediate family. Although she declared her goal was to raise strong daughters, her need for dominance left them dependent on her for everything. She fully supported our education, every one of us earned college and graduate degrees, but three of my sisters returned home, lived under her control, and never made meaningful use of their education.

Rather than celebrating the expansion of her family circle, my marriage and children felt to her like a loss of power. To counter that loss, she inserted herself into my life at critical moments, creating turmoil. For my wedding, she insisted on taking charge of the event in Los Angeles, only to abandon the effort weeks before, leaving chaos in her wake. When I was pregnant and living in Hong Kong with Paul for his Fellowship, she demanded I return alone to Los Angeles and live with her for the arrival of her first grandchild. After all arrangements had been made, and only two weeks before I was due to fly back, she mailed me classified ads directing me to find my own apartment and transportation to the hospital. Once again, chaos.

I came to dread every holiday season, waiting through her endless indecision before I could finalize plans with Paul's parents. Each time, she may have felt more powerful, but in doing so she turned my gratitude into resentment and pushed me further away.

Her obsession with control extended even to the family home. Having lost her original home in the Communist takeover, she became irrationally determined that one of us must always remain with the house. Schucherry, my sister, was most often assigned that role and suffered severe mental health consequences. When she came to San Francisco to serve as a bridesmaid in my wedding, my mother assigned our eleven-year-old sister, Joanne, to stay behind, alone, for the entire weekend, simply to "watch the house."

None of this made sense. But my mother's emotional need for control was all-consuming, undermining the very goals she set for herself and for us.

And as I would later discover, the same dynamic appeared in my professional life.

WORK

In today's world, no industry or company is immune from forces outside its control. Yet when emotions rooted in the need for control take over, they often drive destructive behaviors that undermine success.

I saw this firsthand during the so-called "merger" of Security Pacific and Bank of America. It was an acquisition: most Security Pacific employees would eventually be let go, and management roles would be decided individually. Many employees, at all levels, had the emotional intelligence to focus on what they could control, doing their jobs well. But others, particularly senior managers accustomed to wielding authority, reacted in self-destructive ways. One Security Pacific Executive Vice President repeatedly lashed out at Bank of America management over minor slights, flaunting his title as if it carried weight. Had he acted from logic rather than emotion, he might have recognized that his behavior only destroyed any chance of being considered for a senior role at the new bank.

The same lesson applies to entrepreneurship. Control issues can significantly hinder a company's growth. Founders often achieve early success through vision and hands-on involvement, but an inability to relinquish control can stall their ability to scale. I consulted with several promising start-ups where the leaders recognized the problem. They "talked the talk," setting up management structures and even running teamwork exercises, but when it came to "walking the walk," the founder's inability to let go ultimately held the business back.

Focus on What You Can Change

Constantly fretting over the unchangeable distracts us from what we can control. When my children applied to schools and jobs, they faced bias because they were Asian and petite. I told them, "You will always be Asian, female, or short. If you blame something you cannot change, you hand your power away." Using an immutable trait as an excuse becomes a crutch that stalls progress.

Know When to Move On

Sometimes, no matter how hard you try, conditions are stacked against you. Accepting that truth is not defeat; it is control. I could not rescue my sisters unless they were willing to change. At work, I have left positions where success was impossible because systems were too entrenched. In such cases, it is wiser to seek a place where your efforts can flourish.

Hoping circumstances will magically shift only deepens frustration. Take charge, decide, and move toward a better situation. Your energy is precious; direct it where it can make a real difference.

Reflection Exercise: Reclaim Your Energy

Use this exercise after reading the section on letting go of what you cannot control. Set aside about twenty minutes in a quiet space with paper and pen.

Ground And Breathe (2 minutes)

- Sit comfortably, close your eyes, and take five slow breaths. With each exhale, picture tension leaving your body.

Dump The Worries (5 minutes)

- On one side of the page, list every worry, regret, or "I wish it were different" thought in your mind. Do not censor yourself.

Sort What You Can Influence (5 minutes)

- Draw a line down the center of the page. Move each item to the right side if you have any direct influence over it. Leave the rest on the left.

  - **Influence examples:** skills you can build, conversations you can start, actions you can schedule.
  - **No-influence examples:** other people's choices, past events, unchangeable traits.

Release The Unchangeable (3 minutes)

- For each item left on the "no influence" side, place a small X next to it and whisper, "I release this." Visualize the words floating away like clouds.

Plan One Small Action (3 minutes)

- Choose one item from the "influence" side. Write one concrete step you can take within the next 24 hours to move it forward.

Set A Worry Window (optional)

- If stray anxieties creep in during the day, give them a five-minute slot this evening. Outside that window, remind yourself: "Not now. I will address this later."

Close With Gratitude (2 minutes)

- List three things, however small, that are going well. Read them aloud to anchor your mind in the present.

Repeat this exercise whenever you feel stuck in regret or rumination. Over time, you will train your attention toward actions that matter and free up energy for what truly moves you forward.

Let Go of Regrets and Forgive Yourself

Regret is universal. We can keep punishing ourselves, or we can gather the lesson and move forward.

Growing up, my parents projected their conflicting agendas onto me, leaving me powerless to choose my own course. I became a doctor to satisfy them, then angered them by marrying a man without family wealth. My mother called me foolish for working and "making money for my husband." While juggling a young family and a demanding career, I miscarried. Wracked with guilt, I refused to go to the hospital even as my bleeding became severe. My mother piled on, insisting I had caused the loss through my "stupidity" in working. By the time I finally sought medical help, I had lost three units of blood along with the pregnancy. It took years of prayer and reflection to accept this tragedy as part of God's plan and release the guilt.

I am blessed with two wonderful children. Because my own childhood was harsh, I strove to give them the opposite. I sometimes wonder if I overindulged them, making things too easy, and delaying their growth. Small slights from them felt like proof that I had spoiled them. In the end, I recognized that I cannot change the past. They are adults on their own journeys, and my role now is to offer love and let go.

At work, I cringe when I recall early management blunders. My mother's win-or-lose worldview shaped me, and I often escalated minor disagreements into battles. I used title and position to push my agenda. After several painful setbacks, meditation helped me see that "win-win" solutions feel better and take me farther in the long run. I regret the mistakes, but I cannot erase them. They are stepping-stones that made me a stronger, more empathetic leader. Continual self-reproach would change nothing; growth does.

4

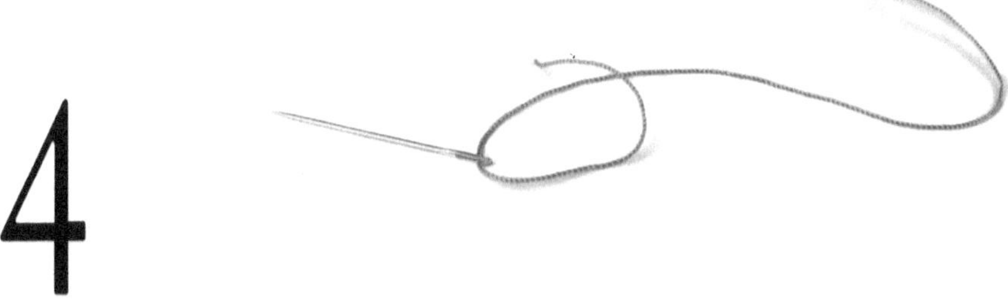

Letting Go of No-Win Situations

SOME DECISIONS FEEL impossible. Whatever choice we make, regret can creep in and tempt us to rehash the alternatives. I have learned that I am human, I act on the best information I have, and once the choice is made, I must move forward.

A Personal No-Win: Confront or Move On?

Sexual harassment in the 1970s often placed women like me in tight corners. Should I fight an injustice and risk derailing my career, or should I move on and refocus my energy? I eventually faced this question head on.

Throughout medical school and residency, unwanted attention was common. I tried to blend in as just another resident, but it was impossible not to stand out as the only woman in a surgical program.

I still remember the anxiety I felt when I was summoned for a meeting with the Associate Department Chair. I braced myself for a critique of one of my surgical cases. Nothing prepared me for the question he asked: how was my marriage holding up, given the demands of residency and being on call every third night?

When I answered that things were fine, he replied that *he* would not be comfortable without his wife in his bed every third night. I was stunned, and furious, but I also just wanted the meeting to end. Keeping my voice respectful, I said, "That problem has never come up in my marriage. Has it ever come up with the male residents and their wives?"

He went silent.

I closed the conversation: "If there's nothing else, thank you for your concern, but there's no need."

Married house staff or faculty would often praise my work, then belittle their own wives in a twisted attempt at charm. I always thought "if their spouses were so terrible, what did that say about them for choosing those marriages?"

The incident that forced my hand came during my sixth year as Director of Emergency Trauma at LA County. The Residency Director proposed a new, formal system in which residents could evaluate faculty. The chief resident, "D," asked to meet privately. I expected a patient-care issue. Instead, he offered a crude deal: if I slept with him, my evaluation would be glowing; if not, he would destroy me on paper and jeopardize my job. Shocked, I dismissed him with, "We are done here."

I reported the incident to the Residency Director, who suggested I must have misunderstood. When I insisted, he implied that my makeup and wearing skirts had invited the proposition. I escalated the complaint to the Department Chair. After hearing both sides, he decided that "D's" evaluation would be omitted from my file. No discipline, no apology, only "Boys will be boys." I felt betrayed.

Emboldened, "D" now bragged that he would write a bad review because I was a "bad lay." Rumors spread, yet I kept showing up for work. Some colleagues offered support; others whispered. My pride pushed me to rise above the noise and focus on work. An esteemed senior woman physician urged me to sue the County and University, arguing that the fight mattered for every woman in medicine. The idea appealed to the fighter in me.

Then another faculty friend cautioned me. I was in my mid-thirties, and he believed my long-term potential was bright. A lawsuit, even if successful, would take years from my career and brand me with scandal, overshadowing my abilities. His logic was sound, yet swallowing the injustice felt like surrendering my principles.

I replayed the dilemma for nights on end. What resonated was my friend's point about reputation. I had fought my entire life to be judged by character and skill, not by gender, ethnicity, or height. Adding a public battle about harassment would give others another label to hold against me. Lawsuits can become bitter and tedious, often pitting you against colleagues you respect. Even if I won, would I feel victorious?

After long talks with Paul, I decided to let the incident blow over and then leave the department. My choice reflected not only this episode but a deeper concern: a culture that allowed a resident to feel such power over a faculty member was no longer a place where I could thrive.

Some criticized me for failing future generations of women. Was I selfish? Did I compromise my values? I accept now that I made the best decision I could with the information and circumstances at the time.

COMMIT AND MOVE FORWARD

Once you choose a fork in the road, stop looking back. Second-guessing breeds self-doubt and weakens your resolve. Rarely is there a perfect answer. Endless "what if" analysis keeps your gaze on the past instead of the path ahead. Decide, commit, and keep walking.

Reflection Exercise: Making Peace with No-Win Decisions

Use this practice to process a past or present choice that feels impossible. Allow 20 to 30 minutes in a quiet space with a notebook.

Settle In (2 minutes)

- Sit comfortably, close your eyes, take five slow breaths. On each exhale, imagine tension leaving your body.

Name The Fork In The Road (3 minutes)

- Write one sentence that captures the decision, for example, "Confront the injustice or leave the environment."

List The Options (3 minutes)

- Create two columns: Option A and Option B. Under each, jot the main potential benefits and costs you saw at the time you made the choice.

Recall Your Information Set (4 minutes)

- Under each option, note the facts, constraints, and emotions that influenced you. Stay in the past mindset; do not add information you gained later.

Identify Core Values (4 minutes)

- On a new page, list the personal values that mattered most in this decision, such as integrity, career growth, or family stability. Put a checkmark next to any value you honored with your final choice.

ACKNOWLEDGE THE OUTCOME (4 MINUTES)

- Write two or three sentences on what happened after the decision. Be factual, not judgmental. If regrets appear, note them without critique.

EXTRACT THE LESSON (4 MINUTES)

- Below the outcome, finish this prompt: "The skill, insight, or resilience I gained from this experience is…" Focus on growth, however small.

RELEASE THE "WHAT IFS" (3 MINUTES)

- Close your eyes, inhale slowly, and picture any lingering doubts as stones in your hands. Exhale as you visualize setting the stones down and walking forward.

COMMIT TO FORWARD ACTION (3 MINUTES)

- Complete this sentence: "When the next tough choice arises, I will remember to…" State one practical way you will apply the lesson you just named.

CLOSE WITH GRATITUDE (2 MINUTES)

- List two things you appreciate about yourself for navigating the situation. Read them aloud to seal the exercise.

Repeat whenever a decision feels like a no-win. Over time, this practice will train your mind to honor your values, trust your past self, and focus on the road ahead rather than the turn you left behind.

5

Making Decisions Out of Fear

FEAR SHAPED MANY OF my early choices. In my childhood, my parents threatened that if I disobeyed or underperformed, I would be cast out to fend for myself. Powerless and terrified, I prized security above all else. They taught me to distrust everyone and imagine the worst-case scenario in every situation.

Looking back, I understand where their beliefs came from. My father, orphaned at seven, survived the Japanese occupation and relied solely on himself to become a doctor. My mother watched her family lose everything when the Communists took over. Betrayal was often rewarded. With no religious faith to soften these experiences, they instilled fear in me and a belief that any missteps would be catastrophic.

Fear at Home

My teenage years were a nightmare. Under constant threat of punishment, I was overwhelmed with learning English; caring for 3 baby sisters; serving my mother while my father was working 24/7; and being responsible for my father's back-office work. Life became so unbearable that I contemplated suicide for months, even researching methods.

When my father tried to marry me off to an older doctor at sixteen, my mother exploded. Having only daughters, she saw the proposal as an insult that implied she was inferior to mothers of sons. She decided I would become a doctor myself, proving our worth to my father and the world. That single decision jolted me awake. For the first time, I saw a future.

Ironically, it took nearly dying for me to realize I had nothing to fear. Although I had no desire to practice medicine, I recognized that God had handed me a lifeline. I seized it. I defied my parents, moved out, and supported myself with menial jobs while attending school. Each step beyond my comfort zone built my confidence and reduced my fear of failure. Mistakes became lessons, not life sentences.

FEAR IN THE FAMILY

My parents feared loneliness and wanted their daughters to stay home. They painted the outside world as dangerous and evil. After I left, they turned my sisters against me, using my struggles as cautionary tales. Three sisters never left home and never married. Two died young from cancer, even though we had no family history of the disease. They missed the joy and growth that come from living fully, all because they clung to fear.

FEAR IN OTHERS

I see echoes of this pattern everywhere. A friend avoids committed relationships, choosing casual hookups to dodge potential heartbreak. A colleague accepts a routine job rather than risk failure by taking on new challenges. Another friend sabotages himself whenever success is within reach. Many people are afraid to ask for what they deserve and continue to settle, whether in love or work.

MOVING BEYOND FEAR

Meditation helps me face fear head on. I ask for guidance and then consider the worst that could happen. If the worst is failure, I remind myself that failure is simply a lesson that propels me forward. Roadblocks are detours, not dead ends.

When making decisions, I examine my motivation. Am I running away from something negative, or moving toward something better? Decisions driven by fear often create new problems, like jumping from the frying pan into the fire. I now strive to choose based on positive goals rather than negative escapes.

Before moving on, take a moment to pull these insights into your own life. Seeing how fear shaped my choices is one thing; spotting where it steers yours is another. Turning a vague sense of unease into concrete questions lets you decide with intention instead of habit. The quick checklist that follows is designed to do exactly that, shine a light on any fear-based thinking, then point you toward one small, courageous step forward.

REFLECTION EXERCISE: FEAR REFLECTION CHECKLIST

Use this quick checklist to spot whether fear is steering your choices and how to pivot toward courage. Keep it handy in a journal or on your phone. Check the boxes that apply, then choose one item to act on this week.

- Am I deciding to avoid a negative outcome rather than to pursue a positive goal?

- Have I pictured the worst-case scenario and honestly assessed whether I could handle it?

- Is this choice driven by other people's approval (parents, partner, boss) more than my own values?

- Am I assuming that one failure would be permanent or fatal to my future?

- Have I identified one small experiment or step that lets me test the waters instead of taking an all-or-nothing leap?

- Do I regularly meditate or breathe to calm my nervous system before making decisions?

- Have I asked someone I trust for a reality check on the risks I see?

- Am I holding on to a safe but stagnant situation because of fear of the unknown?

- Did I run through the question, "What good thing could happen if I say yes?"

- After weighing facts, am I ready to commit and stop second-guessing?

Next Step: Circle one statement that feels important. Set a 10-minute timer today to brainstorm how you can move it toward a checkmark.

6

Setbacks As Opportunities

MUCH OF OUR SELF-IMAGE starts with our parents. Children raised in love and approval usually feel more secure. My parents came from opposite ends of the economic spectrum, yet neither received much affection growing up. Harsh circumstances forced them to view life in stark terms: succeed and live, fail and suffer, even die. Unsurprisingly, they judged me only by results. Growing up immersed in the Chinese traditional culture also cultivated their core belief that children are properties rather than independent individuals.

When I arrived in the United States at eleven, I had attended school in Hong Kong for just six months. I spoke no English and knew little math. My parents had little patience for my slow progress. They called me stupid and incompetent. As a young teenager unable to earn money for the household, I was dismissed as a "fan tun" or "rice bucket," useful only for consuming food.

That conditioning taught me to feel worthy only when I produced. I equated success with survival and saw every setback as catastrophic. Today I recognize that many so-called failures turned into my greatest opportunities, while some early "successes" would have limited my growth. Two career episodes illustrate this shift in perspective.

USC: When A Door Stays Closed, Build Another One

After leaving LA County, I joined the USC Student Health Center. The role let me balance work with a young family. Once the work became routine, I spotted an opportunity: the University spent heavily on employee health benefits, while its Medical School needed more referrals. Drawing on relationships I had built with community hospitals during the Olympics, I designed and executed a University Health Plan that solved both problems. The plan saved USC money while feeding new patients to the medical school to kickstart their new Private Practice.

That success earned me goodwill with both the Dean and the Vice President for Health Affairs. They promoted me from assistant professor to full clinical professor, raising my hopes to leverage my good will into a promotion at the Medical School. I proposed a new Associate Vice-President position that would expand managed-care contracts for the new Faculty practice. I poured myself into a business plan and rehearsed the presentation for weeks. Meetings were pleasant; promises were plentiful. Progress, however, was nonexistent. The Dean "loved" my proposal to add managed-care content to the medical curriculum and forwarded it to the curriculum committee, which I learned later, functioned as a "black hole" for ideas.

A trusted friend from HR finally opened my eyes that the promises were just lip service. USC Leadership was an old-boy network that rewarded harmony over problem solving, and I did not fit the mold. After a short period of meditation (and disappointment), I made a plan to transition from the University. I stayed long enough to secure tenure benefits and finish an MBA, then left academia for the business world.

Six years and two outside positions later, USC tried to recruit me back, this time at full Vice-President level. By then the title no longer mattered. Instead, I agreed to a consulting arrangement, earning ten times what the Associate Vice-President position I coveted would have paid. Had I received the promotion when I wanted it, I might have remained in a narrow lane and missed the growth that followed the setback.

AETNA: A SUDDEN EXIT, A HIDDEN GIFT

With the merger of Security Pacific and Bank of America, I turned down the position of SVP and Corporate Medical Director for the merged bank. Instead, I chose to go to Aetna as Vice President and Corporate Medical Director with the goal of learning the insurance business. The choice meant a lonely journey into a strange environment, a large pay cut, two years of cross-country commuting between California and Connecticut and a strain on my family. I trusted that the potential learnings would be worth the sacrifice.

When I arrived in 1991 at Aetna's corporate headquarters, Aetna was the country's largest national insurer, steeped in tradition and tight community relationships in Hartford. With the Clinton Health Care Reform debate, managed-care pressures were rising, and the Company tried to appear agile by appointing me their Official Spokesperson on Health Reform. Inside, though, the culture resisted change. Job cuts and policy shifts created confusion and fear.

As one of the few senior managers with managed-care experience, I was assigned a key project of human-resources analysis. My business manager arranged a morale-building dinner for department heads. At the end of the evening, she handed me a form and said the department would cover the cost; I signed.

Two weeks later a finance officer told me I was terminated for an unauthorized expense and had three days to clear my desk. I was stunned. I suspected a setup and had failed to appreciate the depth of relationships in the Company. I later learned that the business manager's brother worked in sales, a group that felt threatened by my analysis, and the finance officer was her cousin.

Human resources investigated. Several managers confirmed that the business manager had directed me to sign. HR offered to reinstate me. That night, exhausted, I slept for the first time in days and woke with clarity: it was time to go home. The incident forced a decision I had been postponing. Aetna paid for my move back to California and provided a generous severance.

Being "terminated" felt like failure, yet it spared me further turmoil and protected my marriage from further strain of extended long-distance separation. Over the next three decades Aetna struggled through acquisitions, layoffs, and leadership changes before finally relocating its headquarters out of Hartford to shed the old culture. The lessons I carried, from insurance mechanics to health policy and the politics of entrenched organizations, became assets in later roles and in a successful consulting practice.

Setbacks arrive without warning, but each one can point us toward a wider horizon. If the USC promotion or the Aetna position had worked out as planned, I might have been comfortable, but not fulfilled. Instead, the disappointments redirected me to opportunities that shaped my expertise and my life.

REFLECTION EXERCISE: TURNING SETBACKS INTO STEPPING-STONES

Use this exercise to mine your own disappointments for hidden opportunities, just as the USC and Aetna chapters revealed. Allow 25–30 minutes with pen and paper.

NAME THE CLOSED DOOR

- Write a brief title for one setback that still stings. Keep it to a sentence, for example "Promotion that never came" or "Job lost without warning."

Rewind The Story

On half a page, list the key facts:

- What happened

- Who made the decision

- Your immediate reaction (anger, shock, grief, relief)

Stay factual; save judgments for later.

Spot The Hidden Gifts

Answer these questions in a paragraph each.

- What skill, awareness, or courage did the setback force you to develop?

- Which limiting path did it prevent you from staying on?

- What door opened next that would not have opened otherwise?

Connect to Core Values

- Circle any value the setback nudged you to honor (growth, family, integrity, creativity, impact). If none fit, add your own. Under the circle, write one sentence on how that value shows up in your life today.

Reframe The Narrative

- Complete this statement three times with different angles: "Because that happened, I now _____________."

Examples:

- Approach new roles with clearer boundaries

- Trust my intuition when an environment feels off

- Know my marriage can weather distance

CHOOSE A FORWARD ACTION

- Identify one small step that uses the lesson. It could be updating your résumé, booking an informational interview, or setting a boundary with a current supervisor. Write it down with a date you will do it.

SEAL WITH GRATITUDE

- Close your eyes for one minute and thank yourself for surviving that moment and still showing up. When you open your eyes, list two positive qualities you proved to yourself through the experience.

Repeat this exercise with other setbacks whenever you feel defined by what went wrong. Each time you will uncover fresh evidence that the detour prepared you for the road you are on now.

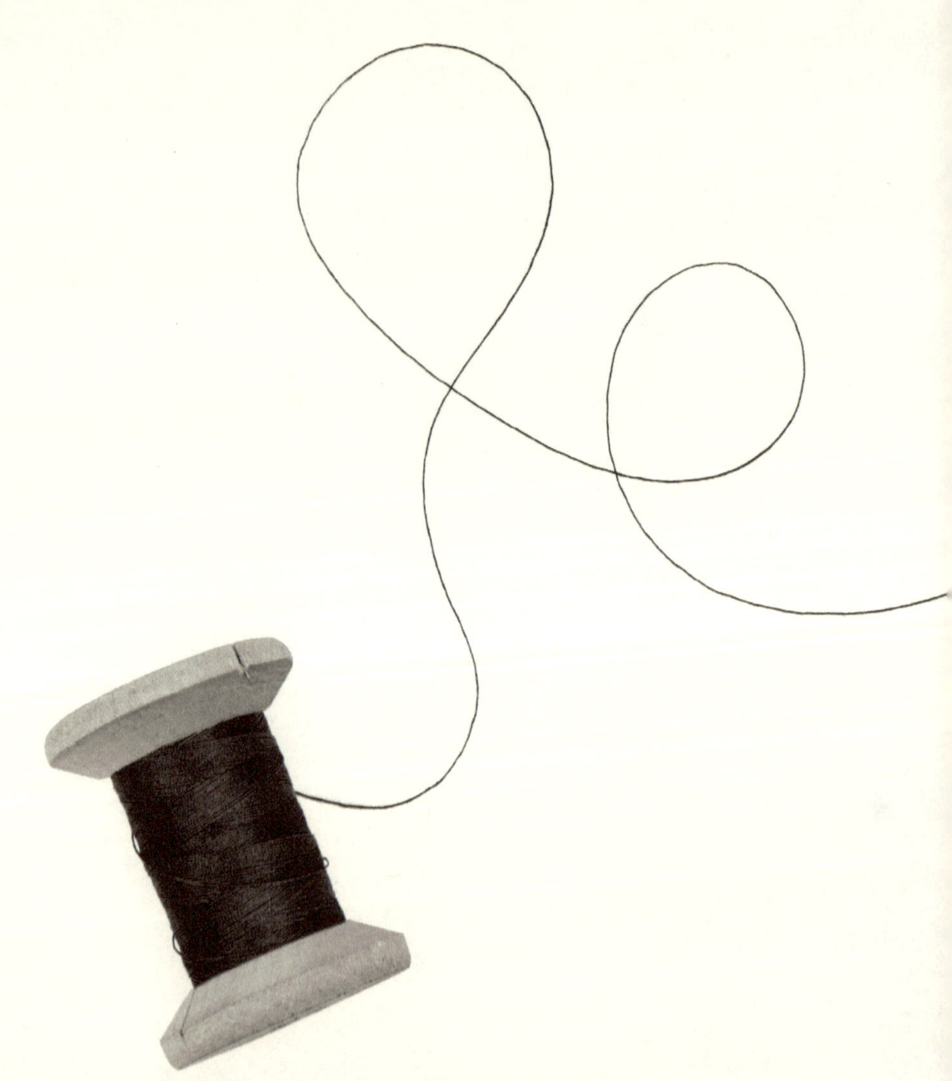

Part Two

Embracing the Positives

7

Positive Company

EACH MORNING, I STAY in bed for about forty minutes and meditate before I do anything else. I begin by thanking God for my blessings, large and small. Next, I replay past moments when divine help carried me through danger or doubt. Then I ask for continued guidance, wisdom, and strength to meet the situations that will unfold today. I close the sequence with slow breathing exercises, inhaling calm and exhaling whatever tension lingers.

When I finally rise, my mind feels clear, my heart feels light, and I can greet the day with purpose.

CHOOSING TO BE POSITIVE

Positivity is a decision, a difficult, deliberate decision that requires steady effort. One of the most powerful tools is choosing the company you keep. Negative people drain energy; positive people inspire it. Surround yourself with those who lift you up and study how they face life.

Hardships by themselves do not define us; our response does. I saw the difference firsthand in my own family.

My mother and my mother-in-law faced nearly identical trials. Both were separated from their husbands for years. Both lost everything during the Communist takeover and had to start anew in the United States. Both had grown up with servants and had never done housework before emigrating.

Yet their outlooks could not have been more different.

My mother clung to grievance. She blamed my father for every loss. She never adjusted to life without servants and instead put me, her oldest daughter, to work as house help. She resented any kind of work as a reminder of her lost wealth and status, once refusing to bring me a glass of water when I lay in bed with a 104-degree fever, telling me, "I am not your servant."

Even after learning that my father's move to America spared us from the Cultural Revolution that killed so many of our former neighbors, she refused gratitude. Bitterness consumed her. She demanded unquestioning obedience, insisting that her daughters revolve their lives around her. Three of the five never left her side.

When I rebelled and moved out, I became the family's enemy. The attitude was I needed to atone for "deserting the family." No repayment was ever enough because I would not surrender my own life for her approval. My mother's world shrank until she had no friends, only resentments.

The contrast taught me a lasting lesson: choosing positivity is not naïve optimism, it is an act of self-preservation and growth. Holding on to bitterness traps us in the past, but claiming a positive outlook, through daily practices, supportive relationships, and conscious gratitude, creates space for healing, opportunity, and joy.

CHOOSING POSITIVE COMPANY

My mother-in-law faced the same losses and dislocations my mother did, yet she chose gratitude over grievance. When she and my father-in-law prepared to reunite in the United States after years apart, she assumed he had become "Westernized." Eager to meet him halfway, she took etiquette and dance classes in Hong Kong, lessons she later laughed about because he was still the same simple man she had married.

Unable to buy familiar foods in their new home, she taught herself to cook full Chinese dinners, even fermenting her own soy sauce and pressing fresh tofu. Friends and family soon prized her meals. She never resented doing the housework that used to be done by her household servants. Instead, she worked to sponsor relatives and friends to migrate to the US and provided support in their early months in the US. She brought her own grandmother over from China when she was 90 years old and took care of her until her passing at 102. Paul remembers those years when his mother was often cooking for 20-30 people every night. She never complained, instead believing that housework and cooking were privileges, proof that God had given her strength to help and serve those she loved.

Wedding Day with New in-law.

By contrast, my own mother saw her life changes only through the negative lens of losses. Time spent with her left me drained. She found fault everywhere. A minor problem became a catastrophe in her telling. If I ever went to her with a problem, it is a guarantee that I will leave feeling ten times worse. Prayer and meditation helped me shed the negativity, but it took years to unlearn patterns I had grown up with. My husband's spirituality and my mother-in-law's radiantly positive outlook became my lifelines. No matter what burden I carried, I felt lighter after talking with my mother-in-law. Her faith was practical: acknowledge the problem, thank God for the chance to grow, and move forward. 15 years after her passing, I still pray for her guidance.

We all know "glass-half-empty" people who recite an endless list of complaints. Their problems are real, yet some seem to thrive on victimhood. I offer help when I can, but if they cling to misery, I step back. Instead, I spend time with friends who view life as "glass half full." They trust that events have purpose and will work out, and their presence lifts me. Our conversations center on blessings, gratitude, and solutions; I leave feeling energized.

Grief offers a clear test. Several friends have lost spouses. All were devastated, yet after a period of mourning, their paths diverged. One woman was widowed suddenly in her fifties. Friends rallied, but ten years later her identity was still "victim." The smallest reminder of her husband could trigger hysterics. People withdrew, tired of her sense of entitlement and wary of saying the wrong thing. Twenty years on, most of those friends are gone.

Then there is "Mom #2," Ann, my college friend's stepmother. I have loved her for more than fifty years. She buried three husbands and a son and weathered serious financial and health blows, yet she greets the world with curiosity and warmth. I once asked how she remains so positive. She smiled, "Schu, I have to, for my sanity and to keep friends. Who would want to come to my pity party? I refuse to grow old, lonely and bitter. That leaves one choice: work at being a positive, fun person to be around."

Visit with Ann in Florida.

We all recognize both types: the perpetual victim who magnifies every setback, and the naturally cheerful soul who faces problems, adapts, and keeps moving. The people we choose to keep close shape our outlook more than any circumstance. Friends, even family, who add light belong in our inner circle; those who pull us into darkness can remain on the outskirts. The choice is ours.

REFLECTION EXERCISE: CHOOSING POSITIVE PEOPLE AND ENERGY

Before you dive into the prompts, pause and look back over the stories of my mother, my mother-in-law, Ann, and the friends who chose very different paths through grief. Notice how each person's perspective shaped not only their own happiness but the atmosphere around them. Your mindset and the company you keep are equally powerful forces in your life. The questions below are designed to help you test where you are right now, who adds light, who dims it, and how you can steer your days toward warmth, gratitude, and growth. Take them slowly, journal your answers, and let each response guide a practical next step.

MORNING GROUNDING

- What simple practice can you add to the start of your day— gratitude, prayer, breathing, that reliably lifts your mood?

ENERGY AUDIT

- Think of three people you interact with most often. After spending time with each one, do you feel lighter, heavier, or the same? Why?

PATTERNS LEARNED EARLY

- Which attitudes from your upbringing still influence how you respond to problems today? Are they serving you or holding you back?

BITTERNESS CHECK-IN

- Recall a recent disappointment. Did you focus more on what was lost or on what might still be possible? What would a "glass half full" response look like?

SUPPORT CIRCLE

- Who in your life embodies practical positivity, acknowledging problems but acting with hope? How can you spend more time with them or learn from their approach?

BOUNDARIES WITH NEGATIVITY

- Is there someone whose constant complaints drain you? What specific, courteous boundary can you set to protect your energy?

ROLE MODELS

- Identify one "Ann" in your world, someone who stays engaged and caring despite setbacks. What habit or mindset of theirs can you adopt this week?

CONTRIBUTION, NOT CONSUMPTION

- When you meet friends or family, do you add light to the room or look for others to supply it? List one way you can bring more encouragement or humor to your next gathering.

Spend a few minutes journaling on each question, then choose one small action to reinforce a positive shift in your daily life.

8

Mindset and Perspective

EMBRACING THE POSITIVE is an intentional practice. It begins with a decision to look for good in every person and situation. We all know hyper-critical voices that hunt for faults. Do you enjoy their company? Neither do I. Constant negativity drags everyone down, so I remind myself daily: none of us is perfect, yet fault-finding blinds us to the "good stuff." My motto remains "Take the best, leave the rest."

Conflicts arise in any relationship. In fifty-five years of marriage, Paul and I have had our share. We are both strong-willed. I prize his steadiness, he is my Rock of Gibraltar, but try moving that rock and you will test your patience. I have a quick temper and my own streak of stubbornness. Over decades we have learned to pick our battles, concentrate on solving the problem, and skip the blame.

Every individual and organization carry flaws. If we fixate on short-comings, we miss the positive contributions. Think of people who radiate cheer: they still face problems, yet they adapt, stay curious, and are a joy to be around. I study them and aim to follow their example. Victim-minded friends who see doom in every turn only add stress. Which path will you choose?

I know which path I choose, and I work at it. Positivity lives in the small moments. Yesterday a shopper rammed my bare feet twice with his Costco cart. It hurt. My first impulse was anger, but I took a breath and decided this would not ruin my day. I turned, smiled, and said, "I'm guessing because I am so short you didn't see me, but you just hit my feet twice and it hurts." He apologized, and I let it go. Maybe he was having a rough day himself. By starting each morning with gratitude and carrying that spirit forward, I refuse to let small irritations turn a good day sour.

9

Morning Meditation Ritual

THIS PRACTICE OPENS every day for me. On workdays, I set my alarm forty-five minutes early so I can complete the sequence before leaving bed. Feel free to adapt the length or wording to fit your own rhythm.

Set The Scene

Stay comfortably on your back, eyes closed. Take one slow breath to signal that the next minutes belong only to you.

Visualize Protective Light

- **White Pyramid** – Picture a pure, white pyramid of light forming around your entire body. See its walls glow with calm strength.

- **Healing Green** – From the palm of your hand, imagine a ribbon of green light circling you once. Let it dissolve into the atmosphere while the white pyramid remains.

Breathing Sequence

With each pair below, inhale the first quality and exhale the second. Repeat each pair once or twice before moving to the next.

- Inhale positives, exhale negatives

- Inhale God's creative energy, exhale doubts and fears

- Inhale good health, exhale toxins

- Inhale relaxation and peace of mind, exhale worries

- Inhale highest good, exhale short-term frustrations

- Inhale prosperity consciousness, exhale scarcity thinking

- Inhale faith, exhale fear

- Inhale love, harmony, and peace, exhale hatred, pettiness, and conflict

Gratitude In Two Layers

General Blessings

- Robust health

- Protection from harm

- Loving, supportive family and friends (name them)

- Abilities to do meaningful work

- Financial freedom to pursue what brings joy

SPECIFIC BLESSINGS

- Natural talents and creative mind

- Guidance away from danger or poor choices

- Healing from illness or accidents

- Lessons learned from past stumbles

Finish by asking for continued protection, guidance, and the grace to use every experience for growth.

AFFIRMATIONS

- I thank my parents for what they gave; I release the harms they caused.

- I forgive myself for my own missteps.

- I silence the voice that says I am unworthy.

- I move forward in freedom, joy, and balance—work I enjoy, leisure, travel, hobbies, family, friends, and faith.

- I welcome God's miracles. I choose understanding over pettiness, calm over anger, and openness over control.

QUIET LISTENING

Let thoughts settle. If guidance or insight arises, note it mentally without analysis.

Seal With Thanks

Repeat a brief thank-you for all blessings, seen and unseen. Open your eyes.

Transition to Action

Rise feeling refreshed and intentional. My own routine continues with a five-mile walk where I review the day's plans. Ideas often surface as I move. However you proceed, carry the meditation's energy into each task, treating the day as both opportunity and lesson.

10

If That Hadn't Happened

LOOKING BACK, I SEE that many hardships were essential stepping-stones. Overcoming adversity forged strength and opened doors that comfort alone could not. Without those trials I would not be who I am today.

Difficult Childhood

Our early years shape us, yet none of us choose our parents, our circumstances, or our family dynamics. Some children grow up in stability. I did not.

I was only eighteen months old when my father left for the U.S. My early childhood unfolded under Communism, without access to education or friends. When my mother told me she was taking me with her, I begged to stay behind with my aunt and grandmother, who had cared for me since I was three. I cried, convinced I was about to lose everything and everyone I loved.

What I couldn't grasp then was how fiercely my mother had fought to take me with her, and how that decision saved my life. The impact of her courage became painfully clear years later, when I returned to my old street in Beijing after China reopened in the late 1970s and learned that very few had survived the Cultural Revolution. Had things gone as I wanted, I likely would not have survived either.

With my younger sister, Schucherry, in Beijing.

Some children grow up with steady love and support. I did not. World events uprooted my mother from a pampered life and forced her into survival mode. I did not meet my father until age eleven. Both parents were strong-willed immigrants struggling in a foreign land, and their focus on survival left little room for my happiness.

My only escape was school. I had been in the United States only three years and was still learning English while trying to keep up in class. The pressure was immense, yet those years taught me crucial skills: quick problem solving with limited resources, efficient multitasking, and strict time management.

Caught between parents who used me as leverage in their own conflicts, I chose academics as my path to freedom. Medicine was not my calling, but becoming a doctor provided a solid professional foundation. The darkness of those years also showed me exactly what I did not want for my future family.

When I married, I turned down a marriage into wealth, instead choosing to work for a true partnership in marriage, united by shared goals rather than a win-lose struggle for control. I aimed to give our children the freedom to be themselves, the security of unconditional love, and a home that felt like a haven, not a warzone. The silver lining of a dysfunctional upbringing was a clear understanding of its impact and a determination not to repeat the cycle.

School photo taken in Jamestown, North Dakota.

Our young family.

Celebrating Stephen's 2nd birthday.

Miss Chinatown: A Gilded Classroom

When my parents pushed me into the Miss Chinatown pageant, my life changed overnight. I went from eating leftovers in hand-me-down clothes to living a real-life Cinderella story. Tailors stitched custom cheongsams, etiquette coaches taught me how to glide into a room, and banquet halls opened their doors. The freshly prepared banquet dishes were delicious, but the greater feast was social: I learned how to read a crowd, make small talk, and put strangers at ease.

My parents viewed the title through different lenses. For my mother it reflected glory and a chance to elevate her; for my father it was a chance to marry me into wealth and elevate the family's position. He urged me to attract the affluent businessmen I met. While dazzled by the glitz, I felt like an ornament. No one cared about my opinions, only my appearance. I worried constantly about stumbling in high heels, saying the wrong thing, or making a mistake, shaming the family. The focus on appearances, status and influence felt artificial, even hollow.

Yet beneath the surface gloss, the experience became invaluable training. I discovered how to converse with journalists, dignitaries, and people from every social tier. Over time I developed my own style of dress, makeup, and presence skills that proved crucial later.

Those presentation skills helped me thrive as Chief Medical Officer for the 1984 Olympics, where I navigated media, politicians, and corporate sponsors. Years afterward, Aetna chose me as its National Spokesperson on Health-Care Reform largely because I could move comfortably in front of cameras and congressional panels.

I did not enjoy the pageant world, but Miss Chinatown turned out to be a decisive building block. What once felt like a gilded cage became a classroom that prepared me for stages I could not imagine at the time.

Being crowned Miss Chinatown.

MENIAL JOBS THAT PAID FOR SCHOOL

When I was accepted to the University of Southern California my parents insisted that I live at home so my household duties for my mother and office duties for my father could continue. I longed for freedom and to live in the dorms. My parents finally agreed, but only if I paid all dorm fees, meals, books, and personal expenses myself and returned every weekend to resume my responsibilities. They covered the five-hundred-dollar tuition each semester with strict conditions. If I dated, missed chores, or failed to gain admission to medical school they would stop paying and I would be out on my own.

Since my weekends were consumed with my duties at home and my father's office, I only had weekdays to earn the money I needed for dorm fees, books, and all incidentals. I took every job available near campus because I had no car. I worked the switchboard, helped in the cafeteria kitchen, served at banquets, and waited tables in nearby restaurants. Many classmates came from wealthy families and looked down on anyone doing that kind of work. I spent every waking hour either earning money or studying. There was no time for dating or fun. My wardrobe came from secondhand shops or hand me downs from dormmates and my meals were whatever the cafeteria offered. At the time I hated the grind and saw only negatives, not appreciating the life lessons of hard work and responsibility. Years later I realized that period prepared me in ways no classroom could.

When I applied for my first position outside academia the setting was Security Pacific Bank, a national institution with over forty thousand employees and a health benefits budget of several hundred million dollars. The new role combined responsibilities as first Vice President and Corporate Medical Director and required oversight of two hundred non-clinical employees. Through the application process, I completed seven interviews in settings that ranged from the cafeteria to executive suites. Months after I was on the job, I asked one manager about the process and how they chose me. He explained that the more than seventy applicants had quickly narrowed to three finalists. On paper the other two possessed stronger Ivy League credentials and experience in managed care. Ultimately, two impressions tipped the scale in my favor.

First, everyone noticed that I connected easily with staff at every level. The leadership worried that a physician might act superior to the support employees and disrupt the culture. During interviews I seemed comfortable bussing my own tray in the cafeteria, responded graciously when a server spilled water on me in the executive dining room, and asked frontline staff for their insights. The panel sensed no inflated ego or phony charm. Second, my history demonstrated creativity and quick thinking, qualities they believed essential in a new managed care program where missteps were inevitable. My ego would not be a problem admitting mistakes and making course corrections as required.

That lesson stayed with me. Small details you barely notice can decide a job offer and unexpected parts of your background can matter most.

The same trait distinguished me later in the pharmaceutical world. In some professional circles physicians behave as though they outrank pharmacists. That attitude followed many of my peers from medical school into practice. My interactions with pharmacists as equals were a major factor in MedImpact Healthcare Systems and Pharmacy Management recruiting me as its Senior Vice President and CMO, and in the University of the Sciences in Philadelphia inviting me to join its Board of Trustees. Those roles gave me insights that set me apart from other physician executives and strengthened my consulting credibility with pharmaceutical companies.

I could never have predicted that mopping floors, answering phones, and waiting tables, would shape the qualities that propelled my career. Yet those menial jobs taught humility, empathy, and adaptability, and they became building blocks for every success that followed.

On the personal side, my respect for hardworking people has enriched every corner of our lives. Paul and I feel at ease with friends from many walks of life beyond our professions. Service providers often go the extra mile because we show genuine appreciation for their efforts. That same attitude shaped our approach to help at home. With no grandparents available, we believed a stable household staff was essential for our children's sense of security. Constant turnover of nannies can unsettle a family, so we made hiring good people and valuing them a top priority.

When caregivers feel like part of the family, they care for children with real affection, and children sense the difference between someone who is merely on the clock and someone who truly cares. Even after the kids grew up, I still needed reliable help to keep the household running smoothly while I traveled for work. Over more than forty years we have had only two housekeepers, each staying until retirement. My experience in menial jobs taught me what it feels like to be unseen and underappreciated. Because I understood the need for respect and recognition, our helpers have felt valued and in turn have cared deeply for our family's well-being.

Another piece of legacy I have come to appreciate, especially while writing this book, is how my children interact with people from all walks of life. Despite their education at "elite" institutions and many friends from "elite circles", neither Lisa nor Stephen has ever shown an elitist attitude, and that has become more apparent to me over time.

On a recent luxury family cruise, I watched Stephen move effortlessly between groups. He was just as comfortable chatting with the ship's crew as he was dining with the company's CEO. At one port, he joined several crew members from India for a meal at a local Indian restaurant, something they found particularly meaningful, given India's deeply rooted caste system. On the same trip, he met a woman at the gym and offered to help with her children so she could finish her workout. She later introduced him to her husband, who turned out to be the CEO of the Cruise line. They invited Stephen to dinner, and the connection has continued since.

We never sat either of our children down to explain the importance of treating everyone as equals. And yet, they do. It is in their instincts, their actions, and the way they carry themselves. That, to me, is a legacy worth noting.

Hong Kong and a Difficult Pregnancy

In theory, two people with so much in common should have had little trouble adjusting to life together. Paul and I shared culture, values, education, and discipline. We understood the demands of each other's work. What we did not account for was that we were also equally driven and strong-willed. Two immovable forces on a collision course.

Paul had grown up with his mother as a full-time homemaker, running the household seamlessly, laundry done, house cleaned, Chinese meals on the table. He never had to think about how much work went into it. I, on the other hand, had been used to focusing only on my own needs. Living together, especially while working in the same hospital, forced compromises both large and small.

The biggest compromise came when I agreed to put my residency on hold and accompany Paul to Hong Kong for his Spine Fellowship, with the understanding that afterward he would move with me to Los Angeles for my training and practice. We thought my year off might be a good time to start a family.

Instead, my exhaustion deepened, and a persistent two-week "period" revealed a more serious truth. The Chair of the OB-GYN department at Hong Kong University quickly diagnosed that I was pregnant and losing the baby. Because of the timing of my immunizations, she advised an abortion. Research on live polio vaccines in monkey embryos had shown long-term neurological spine disorders. The only alternative was to attempt to keep the pregnancy, but that would require three months of total bed rest.

Paul and I talked, and we prayed. We knew this was the most important decision we had ever faced, one that would shape our lives.

In the end, we agreed it was in God's hands, but we would do everything we could to try to save the baby.

For three months, I stayed in bed. With little money and no television, I devoured Agatha Christie mysteries that Paul scoured libraries to find for me. I could barely tolerate food, surviving mostly on tea and crackers. Paul came home every noon to bring me lunch and help me to the bathroom, then returned at night with whatever cafeteria meal he could find. He turned down every invitation to go out until I was well enough to leave the apartment.

In many ways, the sacrifices we made during that time strengthened our marriage. Until then, we had been accustomed to focusing on ourselves. This trial forced us to give, to trust, and to care for one another in a deeper way. That trust became the bedrock of our marriage, the foundation that carried us through fifty-five years of challenges and change.

EMERGENCY MEDICINE: CLEAR THINKING IN A CRISIS

I fell into Emergency Medicine almost by accident. Though stressful, never knowing what might come through the door, I was well prepared for life-threatening situations thanks to my surgery and ENT training. What I could not have anticipated, as head of the trauma unit at the County ER, were the bizarre, unpredictable crises that no training could cover. I can still remember the surge of adrenaline that came with those moments.

Once, in the middle of seeing a patient, I heard a loud scream. A nurse had pulled back the curtain on a female overdose patient and found the EKG technician raping her. Within minutes, I secured the patient, restrained the technician, calmed the nurse, called law enforcement, and contained the disruption so as not to alarm other patients.

Another time, while in a meeting, I heard what sounded like an explosion in the suture room. By the time I arrived, a crowd had already gathered. The ceiling had collapsed; a man, covered in drywall and glass, lay partially on a broken gurney. He was conscious, breathing, and had a strong pulse, though his hip was clearly fractured. My instinct was not only to care for him but to ensure the ER itself could continue functioning. I called security to clear the area, engineering to check for structural damage, gas leaks, or exposed wiring, and Orthopedics to prepare for a patient with a broken hip and possible additional injuries. Within minutes, the ER was stabilized. Only then did I learn the cause: a jail ward patient from the 13th floor had attempted suicide. Instead of reaching the ground, he had crashed through a skylight on the 3rd floor, landing in the suture room, the gurney breaking his fall.

For seven years, I faced volatile and often violent situations like these. Street violence followed victims into the ER, sometimes endangering staff. My repeated requests for metal detectors were denied, even after two gang shootouts that narrowly spared us. In every case, my role was to de-escalate, control the situation, and protect both patients and staff. I also learned how critical public relations and political considerations were in managing the aftermath.

At the time, I often asked myself, *Why me?* Why was I always the one in the hot seat, facing crises and the scrutiny that followed? What I didn't appreciate then was how these years prepared me for future roles in the public eye, at the Olympics, and later at Aetna. Handling crises helped hone my ability to quickly zero in on the key issue in chaotic situations and address problems quickly to minimize both short-term and long-term damage, an invaluable skill in everyday life, management, and consulting.

A Moment of Gratitude and Reflection

Before you turn the page, take a moment to consider how your own respect for the people who keep life running shows up each day. Whether it is the barista who remembers your order, the coworker who handles thankless tasks, or the caregiver who watches your child, these quiet contributions shape the quality of our lives. The short reflection below will help you notice where gratitude is already strong and where a simple change of attitude could deepen trust, loyalty, and ease at home and at work.

REFLECTION EXERCISE:

- Sit quietly for two minutes and list the names or roles of five people whose labor supports your daily routine. Include at least one person outside your social circle such as a driver, cleaner, or delivery worker.

- For each name write one sentence describing how their effort improves your day. Be specific.

- Circle the name beside which your gratitude feels thinnest. Ask yourself what small gesture could show genuine appreciation. This might be a handwritten note, a sincere thank-you, or learning something about their interests.

- Schedule that gesture within the next forty-eight hours and note the date.

- Close the exercise by reading the list aloud and ending with the simple words, "I see you. I value you." Sit for one more slow breath before moving on with your day.

Part Three

Trusting Your Inner Voice

11

Life Changing Decisions

HOW DO YOU USUALLY Make big decisions? Do you poll friends and family? Do you bury yourself in research until the options blur? In an age of endless data those paths feel logical, yet when lives truly pivot, I have found that the quiet nudge inside is the surest guide. Long before I heard the word God, I sensed a presence directing my steps. Sometimes I simply knew.

My scientific training teaches objective analysis and my traditional Chinese upbringing taught deference to parents and later to a husband, but in my deepest choices I have relied on instinct. The following moments show how that inner voice shaped everything that followed.

Leaving Home

Confucian teachings framed children as property devoted to parents for life. Filial piety carried more weight than even the Ten Commandments. In my family, any hint of defiance drew threats of being cast out. Craving security, I obeyed, yet another part of me whispered that I would never survive under those rules. Though I had no formal religion I felt God beside me, telling me I was not wrong for wanting independence. The cost was high. My parents branded me the black sheep and my sisters cheered every setback as proof that disobedience deserved punishment. Even so the fear lifted once I stepped away. I discovered that true security rises inside, not from external approval or promise of a safety net.

Choosing a Partner

During my Miss Chinatown year I met Jeff. He seemed perfect. A nice guy. Handsome, training to be a physician, only son of a wealthy Chinese family, even my parents approved.

Jeff visited me whenever he was in the Bay Area, and early in my second year of medical school, he took me home to meet his parents. Their mansion in Pacific Heights overlooked the city, staffed by more than a dozen servants. Afterward, his mother invited me to lunch a few times, arriving in her chauffeured white Rolls. I still remember the way she wrinkled her nose when I slid into the car, smelling faintly of formaldehyde from Gross Anatomy lab. His mother was always gracious, but I could sense I was not the girl she imagined for her son. Patricia, Jeff's sister, had strained the family by marrying a Caucasian, so there was pressure for Jeff to marry the "right" girl.

By every measure, Jeff seemed to be that "right" guy, handsome, wealthy, intelligent, kind. Everyone reminded me how lucky I was. And yet, I carried a quiet doubt: in this family, with this kind of wealth, would I ever truly be myself?

One small incident stayed with me. We were driving one evening, stuck in traffic as dinner approached. I was starving and just wanted to stop somewhere, but Jeff insisted we wait for a "nice" restaurant. Finally, frustrated, we pulled into a Denny's. The burger hit the spot, and I said aloud how delicious it was. Jeff's reply, "I guess it serves the purpose," landed heavily. It triggered a question that never left me: if he no longer had money, could he adjust?

After a few years, we began planning a life together, a life that promised everything I thought I wanted: no more struggles, financial security, stability. I secured a prestigious internship near him and my parents in Los Angeles, exactly what a girl who prized stability should desire. Yet restlessness crept in. My electives were still open, and my intuition urged me to go somewhere completely different before settling down.

The University of Hawaii offered clinical electives with travel and housing covered. All slots were committed two years in advance but after many phone calls, the coordinator agreed to accept me if I paid my own airfare. Savings from three months of rent and summer jobs covered the ticket. Neither Jeff nor my parents liked the idea, but they could not stop me.

In Hawaii, I tasted my first taste of real freedom, an ocean away from my parents. My electives allowed me leisure time to socialize and date. One afternoon at Queen's Hospital, I waited for an elevator beside an Asian man in white hospital scrubs. Nothing about him was extraordinary, yet I suddenly saw a corona of sparkling light above his head and heard a thought as clear as speech. "Pay attention. This man will matter." His name was Paul Tsou, a third-year orthopedic resident on rotation from UCSF.

We kept crossing paths. Nurses considered him one of the most eligible bachelors on the island, yet he treated me like a kid sister. When he finally asked me out my inner voice told me to cancel another date and go. Our first outing was a Paul original. Lunch at a food stall, a kung fu movie in Chinatown, and an unplanned splurge at a fine restaurant. It felt right. Ten days later, on our fourth date he said, quite casually, I think we should get married. I asked why. He answered, we fit. Love was implied, not proclaimed.

On paper, Paul was the wrong choice. He had no wealth, no social standing for my family, and we hardly knew each other's relatives. My parents dismissed him outright. Yet inside, my certainty was unshakable. I didn't analyze it, I simply knew who he was, without needing external validation.

Paul was immovable against outside influence. That strength celebrated my successes, even when colleagues made snide remarks about his "needing a wife to work." That strength allowed him to make sacrifices so I could pursue opportunities. And that same strength, over the years, shaped the values we passed on to our children.

Recently, they gave him a Father's Day card that said: *"When we were young, we used to think you not caring what others thought was weird. Now we think it's awesome."*

I broke off my relationship with Jeff, declined the prestigious Los Angeles training program, and scrambled to find a surgical internship in the Bay Area. Four months later Paul and I married. We have just celebrated our fifty-fifth anniversary. I remind our children that selecting a life partner shapes every day that follows. In that decision trust your inner voice.

The pattern is clear. Logic, culture, and outside opinion have their place, but the compass that never fails rests within.

Wedding and 50th Anniversary Vow Renewal
Stanford Memorial Church.

My Health Crisis

For most of my life I worked long hours without giving a thought to fatigue or wellness. In my thirties I began feeling drained, and a rash crept across my skin. I blamed leftover stress from the Olympics and kept going. When the rash spread and exhaustion deepened, I finally saw the most respected dermatologist in Santa Monica. His verdict stunned me. I had a full-blown autoimmune disorder with a fifty percent chance of death. He urged immediate hospitalization and a two-week course of intravenous steroids.

Fear swept over me. Our children were still small. Paul urged me that treatment would solve everything. I worried that heavy steroids would suppress symptoms but would also weaken me. My joints and bowels soon joined the revolt while I clung to my job. I prayed, meditated, and waited for clarity. One morning I woke with a calm certainty that I should consult a Chinese herbal doctor.

At lunchtime I wandered around Chinatown until I found a modest herbal shop whose sign promised a doctor inside. Dr. Xi had recently emigrated from Shanghai and practiced traditional Chinese medicine. After a long history he examined my tongue and pulse, then explained that my entire system was "off-balance" and every organ was inflamed. Restoring balance would take months of brewed herbs and strict monitoring. Symptoms would likely worsen before they improved. I must also eliminate all caffeine, alcohol, and seafood until I restore balance. If I would commit fully, he would begin treatment; Otherwise, we should not start. My inner voice said YES.

The regimen was grueling. Twice daily I brewed and swallowed bitter decoctions while my skin flared and my energy sagged. I kept the faith. Six months later the disease had vanished. Paul and I celebrated at Rose Café with my first cup of coffee in six months. I believe God guided me to that tiny shop and saved my life.

Rethinking My Career

In the traditional Chinese culture, parents expect children to fulfill family ambitions, with sons often carrying on the family business. My mother decided that her eldest daughter would take the son's role and carry on my father's practice. That meant medicine and, eventually, plastic surgery. I entered surgery and an ear, nose, and throat residency but dreaded surgical days. Hours were brutal, call nights came every third night, and Lisa caught one virus after another in her infancy. Paul focused on his own practice and dismissed my mounting strain. My weight dropped to ninety-seven pounds.

One morning I woke up, asking myself why I was doing this. I disliked the work and saw no joy in a surgeon's future. I made the decision to resign from the program, fully aware that my parents and Paul would protest. My parents refused to speak to me. Paul said he was disappointed that I lacked the character to finish what I started. Friends thought I was crazy to abandon years of sacrifice and the honor of being the first woman in that prestigious program. I held my ground and walked away with no plan. Yet listening to intuition led me into healthcare industry management and strategy, a field that became my professional home and a source of deep satisfaction.

12

Activating Your Inner Voice

THESE CHOICES FRIGHTENED me. Each time I doubted myself, but every leap strengthened trust in that quiet guide. I ignored the many "shoulds" that came from culture, family, mentors, and even my science education. I left my parents' home despite Confucian doctrine, refused to marry for money although friends insisted I was lucky to have the chance, chose Paul when others thought I could do better, declined intravenous steroids in favor of foul-tasting herbs, and quit lucrative posts when mentors urged me to stay.

It isn't only the big decisions. That inner voice guides me every day in "doing the right thing." It is easy to rationalize self-serving choices as the right thing, but deep down, we know when we are ignoring that quiet truth inside.

Each small decision I made by listening to that voice shaped the person I became. At times, it meant giving up short-term gains, but I have never regretted those choices, because I *knew*.

I believe that the inner voice is God's voice. I never go against it. When life demands a difficult choice remember that the wisdom you need already speaks inside you. Listen to it and you will find the path meant for you.

REFLECTION EXERCISE: INNER VOICE ACTIVATION

Before you move on, pause and recall a moment when a quiet nudge inside steered you in an unexpected direction. Perhaps it whispered when logic said stay or spoke up just before you signed a contract. The stories you just read show how that inner compass can override fear, culture, and even professional training. Your own guidance may not arrive as halos of light or clear sentences, yet it is always present. The short practice below is designed to help you recognize that voice, separate it from noise, and give it room to lead.

- Find ten minutes of privacy. Sit comfortably, close your eyes, and place one hand over your heart.

- Take five slow breaths. With each exhale imagine releasing other people's expectations. Feel your shoulders drop and your jaw soften.

- Bring to mind a current decision, large or small. State the choice in a single sentence, as if you were explaining it to a friend.

- Picture two doors in front of you. Behind Door One is the path of pure logic and outside advice. Behind Door Two is the path your body and intuition would choose. Notice which door your attention drifts toward without forcing an answer.

- Open the door that draws you. Allow images, emotions, or brief phrases to surface. Do not analyze them. Simply observe and breathe.

- When the scene fades, place both hands on your heart and ask, what one action can I take this week that honors this guidance. Wait in silence until a word, picture, or feeling appears.

- Write down the action and schedule it. End by saying aloud, I trust the wisdom within me.

Return to this exercise whenever doubt grows loud. Over time the inner voice will speak more clearly and you will step forward with calm conviction.

Part Four

Insights From Career

13

Opening Doors

WHILE I WAS WRESTLING with the decision to leave surgical residency, Los Angeles County–USC Medical Center began building a brand-new Department of Emergency Medicine. Applicants were scarce and the chair offered me leadership of the Emergency Trauma Division. I was twenty-nine and wanted nothing more than predictable hours for my young family and a steady income to repay the three-thousand-dollar down payment loan we had accepted from our parents for our first house. Like many physicians of that era, I assumed management roles were soft positions reserved for doctors who could not or would not practice real medicine. I expected a breather from endless exams and overnight calls. I could not have been more wrong. During the next seven years that supposedly easy job tested me in ways my medical training never did, set my career on a new trajectory, and opened doors I did not know existed.

In the nineteen seventies health-care management roles were almost entirely inside hospitals, and those posts were held by white men. As a minority woman I had no footsteps to follow and no mentors to guide me. I learned by observing, making mistakes, working hard, doing what felt right, and listening to the quiet guidance inside. That method carried me from Academics to Business, from Policy to Media Relations. My titles eventually included Clinical Professor of Medicine and Pharmacy, Medical Director of Emergency Trauma for Los Angeles County, Chief Medical Officer for the 1984 Olympics, VP Corporate Medical Director and First Vice President at Security Pacific Bank, VP and Corporate Medical Director at Aetna, Senior Vice President for Strategic Development and Chief Medical Officer at MedImpact Pharmacy Benefits Management, and Chief Executive Officer of MedDirect Data Informatics. I represented Aetna as its official national spokesperson during the debate on the Clinton health-reform plan, then used the experience and relationships gathered through those years to launch a thriving consulting practice for Fortune 500 companies and start-ups alike.

Every step required trusting instincts, meeting new challenges, and adding fresh skills to an ever-expanding tool box. The insights that grew from those experiences shaped my progress and I offer them here in the hope that they will serve your own path as well.

14

Organization and Culture

WHEN YOU SCOUT A NEW position, where is your focus? Do you focus mainly on title, salary, or perks? Those matter, yet I have learned to weigh something less obvious, the cultural fit.

Early in my management life I thought culture referred only to ethnicity. My first administrative role at the County hospital felt seamless because I had trained there and never questioned the environment. Culture became painfully clear when I moved across town to direct the Student Health Center at the University of Southern California.

Leaving County trauma to go to managing a Clinic was like slamming on the brakes. The fast track of critical care shifted to a cautious, consensus pace. At the County I managed rotating residents in a perpetual sprint. At the clinic I supervised long-tenured employees, from physicians, nurses to ancillary staff, who filled slow hours with gossip. My predecessor was a gracious Japanese American lady physician whom everyone adored. Both of us being Asian female physicians was where the similarities ended. Fortunately, my boss Allan, was patient with my missteps. I thought I was merely carrying out the stated mission to streamline operations and improve quality. The staff saw a bull in a china shop. Changes they considered disruptions were, to me, obvious improvements. I later learned, in that culture, I had been labeled the problem.

After I designed and implemented a program that pleased senior leadership across the University and saved the University millions of dollars, I received plenty of accolades but not the expected promotion. A trusted friend forced me to see the truth. My direct style clashed with a campus culture that prized harmony, political expediency, and keeping problems under wraps. As a minority woman, advancement into the old-boy hierarchy was unlikely. The University would not likely change. I could either adapt or look elsewhere. I chose elsewhere.

From that point on I treated culture as a critical checkpoint. Security Pacific Bank valued clear targets and rewarded results. Aetna was more like a public university – bureaucratic, layered, political, and connection driven with roles and turfs clearly defined. MedImpact was a start-up that thrived on improvisation, and roles stretched to fill gaps as needed. Consulting honed my sensitivity to these informal forces and, when I re-entered the job market, culture guided every conversation.

One example stands out. In the late nineteen-nineties, the top technology company in the world courted me to lead its push to develop a standard information technology platform for health care. The idea thrilled me. I could learn an entirely new field and perhaps help modernize medicine. The company's culture was pure technology optimism. Leaders believed their software would conquer health care as easily as it had reinvented back-office business.

I raised simple business questions. Insurers profit from float, so why would they invest in faster claims payment. Patient privacy rules might restrict open data exchange. Each time, the executives' eyes glazed and they steered back to the magic of code. My instincts warned that this culture lacked the patience to untangle health care's workflow, regulation, and misaligned incentives. I returned for three rounds of talks, tempted by the vision, yet finally declined.

Despite decades of technological progress, conflicting incentives and entrenched workflows remained formidable barriers to adopting electronic medical records. In the end, it took both carrots and sticks, Obamacare regulations paired with the lure of easier upcoding with higher reimbursements, to finally drive the industry to widespread adoption of IT.

This affirms my rule: Before you accept a role, understand how the organization thinks, what it values, how it makes decisions, and whether that rhythm matches your own. The right fit will amplify your strengths. The wrong one will grind them down no matter how shiny the title or attractive pay.

Change never stops. When markets shift, cultures must follow, yet the organizations that once led the field often resist most fiercely. The old insurance culture at Aetna was woven so tightly into Hartford that it took thirty years, multiple leadership shake-ups, and finally a move to New York City before managed-care thinking could take root. Ron Compton, the CEO, once lamented to me that Aetna had spent over tens of millions of dollars on recruitment and consultants in unsuccessful efforts to align the Company with the marketplace. Physicians have also watched private practice give way to salaried posts in large systems. Private-equity ownership is again rewriting group practice expectations. Culture is the current underneath every policy, and it shapes whether new ideas take hold or are quietly killed.

Treat culture as a core factor in any job hunt. Success and day-to-day happiness depend on the fit. Ask yourself whether the environment will let you thrive and whether your style will truly help the organization. If you are recruited to spark change, be sure the company is genuinely committed to change. Remember, the people who built the box usually cannot think outside it.

REFLECTION EXERCISE: CULTURAL FIT SELF-REFLECTION

Sit with a journal and write short answers to these questions about yourself

- Do you prefer a quick sprint pace at work or a measured steady rhythm?

- Are you excited to climb a single corporate ladder or to move across companies for growth?

- Do you thrive in detailed structure or looser frameworks?

- Is creating new ideas and being rewarded for them essential to you?

- Do you enjoy political navigation or find it exhausting?

- Do you want daily learning and professional development?

INVESTIGATE A PROSPECTIVE EMPLOYER

- Study the backgrounds of senior leaders. Finance, Sales, Marketing, Government Relations, or Technology. Their roots reveal the company's true priorities.

- Note tenure. Who rose from within and who arrived from outside. Where did new hires come from and what results followed them.

- Observe diversity in age, gender, discipline, and viewpoint. Uniform groups signal limited perspective.

- During your visit watch how people dress, speak, and interact. Formal suits, relaxed jeans, or mixed styles each tell a story.

- Ask your interviewer how long they have been with the company and what keeps them there. Listen for genuine enthusiasm or polite phrases.

- Inquire an example of a recent company success and how it was celebrated. The answer shows what the organization values.

- After you leave, scan your body. Did you feel energized or tense in those halls? Your physical response is a data point as real as any spreadsheet.

Compare Notes

- Place your self-portrait beside what you learned about the organization. Where do values and habits align? Where do they clash? If the gaps are wide, ask whether adaptation is possible or if another setting will let you give your best work without constant friction.

Return to this exercise each time a tempting title or salary crosses your path. A brilliant position in the wrong culture soon feels like a cage, while the right cultural match can turn even an ordinary title into a springboard for growth and satisfaction.

15

Position and Role Inside The Organization

MOST PEOPLE SCAN AN organizational chart and assume the higher the box the greater the importance. A better question is where the role sits in relation to the company's core business. Is the job part of revenue generation or is it a cost center that supports those who generate revenue? Answering that single question clarifies how leadership will measure your value. If you bring money in, your mandate is simple: grow the business. If you sit on the cost side, your task is to lower expenses and protect the profit engine. Misreading that balance can derail even the brightest career.

When I treated patients, my work was the product that kept the lights on. The day I stepped into Security Pacific Bank as 1ˢᵗ VP and Corporate Medical Director, I occupied a lofty box on the chart, yet my new mission was pure cost containment. The title sounded grand, but I existed to keep the workforce healthy and medical spending low. My success was measured by how I met specific financial targets contributing to the company's bottom line and smooth functioning of the core business. When I exceeded the financial targets set by the CEO, handing him rebate checks from the insurance company totaling millions of dollars in savings, while maintaining employee relations with no unions or lawsuits, I was formally recognized by the Executive Management Team for my contributions.

After Security Pacific announced a merger with Bank of America, my boss was appointed to head Legal and Human Resources at the newly merged Bank and one of top 5 officers on the Executive Management Team. She wanted to reward me with a promotion at a much higher pay at the new Bank of America. On paper it was a coup, but I sensed the merged leadership needed every ounce of attention on integrating the core banking lines. Innovative ideas from a support function would be viewed as a distraction. My compensation would outstrip the savings and value I could realistically deliver. In merger politics I would become a liability for my sponsor. Recognizing that, I declined the coveted post and negotiated a graceful exit that helped both of us. In appreciation, my boss granted me a severance I technically wasn't entitled to, since I had left voluntarily.

A friend of my daughter provides another cautionary tale. He left private law practice to become general counsel at a major hospital. The org chart placed him just under the chief executive, and he assumed that raising every potential legal issue would prove his worth. In law-firm life those red flags create billable hours, but hospital executives heard only higher risk and cost. He lost the job within a year and is still hunting for work. He forgot that his role existed to reduce liability, not to inflate legal activity and his own importance.

The same blind spot trips medical directors in insurance companies. Their real assignment is risk management and reducing claim costs, no matter how lofty the rhetoric about quality. Those who enforce policy so rigidly that they anger actuaries, general counsels, sales, or public relations soon find themselves unemployed. A chief medical officer at a device company may rank near the top, yet the salesperson, not even on the organizational chart, who lands large contracts often wields more power because revenue speaks louder than title.

I was fortunate at Aetna to move from medical oversight into health-reform policy and later at MedImpact into strategic development and sales. Those expansions pulled me closer to the revenue engine and gave me broader influence. I now mentor physicians to seek similar shifts toward the core business whenever possible.

Expanding your role expands your growth. "It's not my job" thinking only limits opportunity. Stepping beyond the job description can be a gift, opening doors to learn about the company and the business in ways you never expected.

When I joined MedImpact, it was a small start-up pharmacy benefits management company with only a handful of employees. No matter our titles, we were all part of sales. The founder was accustomed to everyone going directly to him. When the company grew to 300 employees, I convinced him we needed a management infrastructure with formal planning and accountability. After a couple of false starts with others, he finally said to me, "Just do it," since it had been my idea.

Although I had held several line management roles with financial accountability, I had never built a variance reporting structure, one that required each department to project performance and be accountable for results. It was far outside the usual responsibilities of a medical director. But through painstaking meetings with every department to develop metrics, I not only created the structure, but I gained clarity on how the dollars flowed and the industry's complex business model.

That hard-won understanding of the PBM business later distinguished me in consulting, giving me the insight to develop business and marketing strategies for pharmaceutical clients.

Misunderstanding the true mission of a department can also create issues. Employees often treat Human Resources as an employee advocate who will correct injustice. Despite its lofty mission, HR's true mandate is to promote and protect the organization, reduce turnover costs, and limit liability. Even when a complaint ends with a supervisor's dismissal the motive is corporate self-protection, not personal vindication. Employees who celebrate a victory in HR may discover they have acquired a new label: potential risk.

A brilliant female physician once sought my advice after she filed repeated gender-bias complaints at her staff-model HMO. She won on paper, gaining small victories, but still faced two years before retirement and a lucrative pension. I warned her that her victories carried a price. She needed to rebuild trust with her boss or risk subtle retaliation that could push her out early, derailing her retirement and losing her pension. She swallowed her pride, repaired the relationship, and reached retirement intact.

Whether you are evaluating a new offer or navigating between internal departments, look beyond titles and stated missions. Ask how the role contributes to the organization's financial goals. See other departments through that same lens. When you understand who drives revenue, who contains cost, and how each unit measures success, you can align your efforts, frame your proposals, and protect your career.

REFLECTION EXERCISE: LEDGER-LINE EXERCISE

Pause and map your own position the way I had to map mine. Titles and reporting lines hint at power, but the true measure of influence is how your work touches the company's income statement.

Are you part of what brings cash in, or do you protect and stretch the cash that others generate? The short exercise below will help you see your current or prospective role through that sharper financial lens and reveal where you might adjust your focus, language, or alliances to create greater value.

- Write the name of your current job, or the role you are considering, at the top of a blank page.

- Draw two columns. Label the left column "Revenue Generators" and the right column "Cost Managers."

- List every routine task you perform (or expect to perform) in the appropriate column. If a task serves both functions, place it where most of your time or impact falls.

- Circle three tasks that senior leadership tracks most closely. Ask yourself which metrics are tied to those tasks: new sales, renewal rates, medical-loss ratio, overtime expense, or something else.

- Beside each circled task write one sentence that explains how your work either grows revenue or protects profit. Keep the sentence in plain financial language. If you struggle to do this, note where you need more clarity from your manager or mentor.

- Review the page. Does your daily effort align with the company's main financial priorities? If not, choose one circled task and draft a single action you will take this month, perhaps proposing a process tweak, partnering with a sales colleague, or quantifying the savings your project delivers, to move your work closer to the ledger line that leadership cares about.

- Schedule that action on your calendar, and share your intent with someone who can keep you accountable.

Repeat this exercise every six to twelve months or whenever you consider a new opportunity. Seeing exactly where you sit on the income statement will guide smarter career moves and smoother relationships across departments.

16

Compensation: Valuing Your Worth

THROUGHOUT MY CAREER, I never made money the central issue, but I always insisted on being compensated fairly.

When accepting a position, I negotiated my compensation upfront to align with market rates. Once in the role, I didn't ask for more when responsibilities expanded. Depending on the organization, recognition came through bonuses, added opportunities, or other forms of acknowledgment. The key was establishing fairness and respect from the start.

In consulting, I set my hourly rate and charged every client the same. I never negotiated it. Retainers could vary, but they were always structured around that same rate plus a premium to be available as needed. Retainers provide steady income but come with the tradeoff of being on call to meet a client's needs. I try to limit myself to no more than two retainer clients at a time, occasionally three at most. When more than two "fire drills" happen at once, there is only so much I can realistically manage without compromising quality.

In an era prior to Zoom, client meetings were limited to phone calls or in-person meetings. I charged a 50% rate for door-to-door travel time. Even with that deterrent, I gained the highest status on several airlines. Consistency built credibility, and it made expectations clear on both sides.

When asked to take on extracurricular work, teaching, speaking, moderating forums, or serving in government capacities, I insisted on being paid the standard rate. I never did it "for free." At USC, for example, I insisted on being compensated at the university's standard rate for teaching, even though the pay was nominal, and I donated far more than I received. Payment was not about the money; it was about principle.

I believe that people rarely value what they do not pay for. Insisting on fair compensation is not about greed; it is about mutual respect, accountability, and the recognition of value. Knowing your worth sets the tone for how others will treat you, and how you treat yourself. It is an act of integrity, not entitlement.

Integrity and trustworthiness mean working at all times for the benefit of your boss or clients, not playing games or pursuing hidden agendas for your own gain. In consulting, it is easy to get drawn into politics, to play one person against another, or to share market intelligence between competitors. That is a slippery slope and one I have always avoided.

One reason I was able to command premium retainer rates was because clients could count on me to step in, creatively address the issue, and put out fires quickly, not to take advantage of chaos and turn it into more billable work.

It is also critical to understand the political landscape and recognize where the minefields are. My job was to help position my client well within that landscape, not to use those dynamics to create more opportunities for myself. The larger the organization, the more complex, and consequential, those politics become.

Before moving forward, take time to reflect on how you define and demonstrate your worth. Compensation is not only about numbers; it is a reflection of how you value yourself and how you teach others to value you. The goal is not to chase money, but to build credibility through fairness, consistency, and integrity. These exercises are meant to help you examine your mindset, your habits, and the principles that shape the way you approach opportunity and reward.

Reflection Exercise: Valuing Your Worth

These exercises are designed to help you assess how you position yourself for fair compensation, align your decisions with your values, and build credibility through integrity and foresight.

As you are going through the exercise, keep in mind: credentials alone do not translate into compensation, the credentials must add value to the job at hand.

A vivid example: In the 1980s, Paul and I naively bought a car wash with no idea how to run a small business. We often scrambled when staff didn't show up, especially the cashier. At one point, I asked my sister Arlene, who had completed college, dentistry, and law degrees but was not working, to fill in until I could find someone reliable. She cashiered for seven hours and then sent me an invoice for $2,100, explaining that her rate was $300 an hour because of her degrees.

When I tried to explain that I was happy to pay $15 an hour, twice the going rate, but not $300 since her education was not relevant to the job, my mother sided with her, insisting that someone with that level of education should command that rate. There was no reasoning with them. We paid the $2,100, but never asked for her help again.

Incidentally, Paul and I were regularly the ones cashiering and cleaning bathrooms ourselves, our MD degrees didn't matter one bit there.

Understand The Context

Before you negotiate, reflect on the culture of the organization.

- Is it open and flexible, or more bureaucratic and rule-bound?

- How do decisions get made?

- Where is there room for discussion, and where is there not?

Remember: You can ask for anything, but the ask reflects on you. If it is not feasible within the structure, it puts your judgment in question.

CHOOSE THE RIGHT TIMING

Negotiation belongs after you have been offered the job, not before.

- How might your timing affect perception?

- What message do you want to send about your priorities and professionalism?

Confidence is knowing when to speak, and when to wait.

ASSESS SHORT-TERM VS. LONG-TERM VALUE

Every opportunity carries both immediate and future value.

- Does this position offer you experience, access, or learning that could outweigh a short-term pay cut?

- How does this role fit into the larger arc of your career?

- Are your personal finances structured to give you that flexibility?

I sometimes accepted less pay for roles that offered growth. Paul and I kept our fixed expenses low to preserve freedom of choice.

INVENTORY YOUR VALUE

Take an honest look at your credentials, experience, and distinctive skills.

- What sets your contribution apart from others in your field?

- What unique perspective or track record do you bring that no one else can offer?

- Once you have identified your strengths, research market rates and determine which of your qualities justify a premium.

At the time, no other consultant had managed on every side of the healthcare system. That breadth of experience became my differentiator. It allowed me to help clients translate complex data into meaningful benefits for their various stakeholders, an essential step for gaining market access and driving utilization of their products and services. This unique expertise distinguished me and generated a diverse client base including hospitals, medical groups, insurers, pharmaceutical manufacturers.

However, tangible differentiation alone cannot sustain continued success. It often fades over time as the knowledge becomes disseminated and commoditized.

QUANTIFY THE INTANGIBLES

Trust, political awareness, and good judgment are intangible, but invaluable and most durable.

- What are the intangibles you bring to your work? How do they reduce risk or add stability for your clients or employer?

- Try to assign a value to them, perhaps a 25–50% premium above the market rate.

My clients knew they could trust me not to play all sides. They relied on me to help them navigate internal politics as well as position effectively in the external marketplace. That reliability, and the sense of stability it brought, became an essential part of my value.

Maintain Consistency And Integrity

Decide early how you will approach pricing and client communication, it sets the tone for every relationship that follows.

- Are your rates consistent across clients?

- How do you communicate changes clearly and transparently?

- Have you ever been tempted to discount or overbill, and what might the long-term consequences be?

Discounts spread quickly. Once you start, it's hard to stop. Hold your line with respect, confidence, and clarity.

Weigh Reputation Over Revenue

Every interaction influences how others perceive your integrity.

- Would you rather be known as opportunistic, or as trustworthy?

- What message do your rates, consistency, and communication send about your professionalism?

Some consultants padded their hours. I never did. My clients recognized the honesty behind my higher rate, and valued it all the more.

Align Compensation With Integrity

- Do your financial decisions reflect your values?

- How do you balance fairness to yourself with fairness to others?

- Where might you need stronger boundaries or greater clarity in future negotiations?

Knowing your worth is not about demanding more, it is about standing in your principles and leading with integrity.

Part Five

Insights from Career

17

Management

PEOPLE HAVE WRESTLED with the puzzle of leadership for thousands of years. In the nineteen-fifties business scholars formalized the idea, defining management as "the function of getting things done through others." Peter Drucker accelerated that thinking with his Management by Objectives model, and since then shelves have been filled with books on how to do it right. My own MBA came after I had already sat in several leadership chairs, so I relied as much on instinct as on any textbook rule. To me, management is an art informed by science. It is also three-dimensional. You must guide the team that reports to you, support the leaders you report to, and collaborate with peers inside and outside the organization. What follows is not a review of theories but hard-won lessons from the front lines of my own career.

18

Managing Down

TITLES, RESPECT, AND REAL LEADERSHIP

A lofty title and a corner office look like the high point of achievement, but I learned quickly that respect does not ride in on a nameplate. Leadership exists only if people choose to follow.

I was still shy of thirty when I stepped into Los Angeles County USC Medical Center as Director of Emergency Trauma. On my first morning the attending physicians, residents, and nurses greeted me with polite skepticism. I was the only woman and the only minority among them, which fed every hidden insecurity I carried. Jeff Sipsey, a seasoned physician already known as the department's anchor, had no interest in answering to a new boss, especially a woman a foot shorter than him. With well-honed sarcasm he turned staff laughter against me whenever he could.

I wanted to stamp my foot and announce, "I am in charge," but that would have confirmed their worst assumptions. Instead, I worked alongside the team. I took the night shifts nobody wanted, cleaned gurneys when orderlies were stretched thin, and asked nurses for their insights before issuing directives. I watched how Jeff spoke to patients and staff, then adjusted my own style. Gradually people saw that every policy I set grew from the same ground-level challenges they faced.

I set out to prove myself, not just to them, but to myself. I reverted to what I had always done when facing resistance: I worked harder than anyone else.

Jeff had a sharp, sarcastic humor that kept the room laughing, usually at my expense. No matter what I said or did, it only seemed to feed the perception that I didn't belong. I made a silent promise to myself that I would not give him the satisfaction of seeing how deeply it hurt, but it did. There were many days I held it together through my shift, only to cry in the bathroom or on the long drive home.

Rather than trying to command respect from above, I met staff at their level. I rolled up my sleeves and made it clear that no task was beneath me. My decisions came from a place of shared experience, not detached authority. I also paid close attention to Jeff, how he interacted with patients, how he earned trust. I made small but deliberate shifts in my own approach.

It did not happen overnight. In fact, it took nearly two years of consistent effort before something changed. Staff who had once ignored or challenged me started coming directly to me with problems and ideas. That shift, quiet but unmistakable, was the moment I knew I had earned their respect and recognition as their leader.

Here is a brief reflection exercise to help you evaluate your own leadership presence, especially if you are in a position where authority alone is not enough.

LEADERSHIP WITHOUT THE TITLE: A RESPECT CHECK-IN

Take a few minutes to reflect on the following:

- How do you show you are part of the team? What is one recent moment where you rolled up your sleeves and worked alongside your staff or peers?

- How do you handle resistance? Is your first instinct to push back, shut down, or lean in and listen?

- What is one behavior you admire in someone who has earned genuine respect in your workplace? How might you begin to model that behavior in your own way?

- Are people bringing problems and suggestions to you unprompted? If not, what small step can you take this week to build more trust and open communication?

Leadership is not about proving your power, it is about earning trust. Use this check-in anytime you are feeling unseen, unacknowledged, or unsure how you are showing up.

CHIEF MEDICAL DIRECTOR, 1984 OLYMPICS: LEADING THROUGH INFLUENCE

In the early 1980s, Los Angeles prepared to host the Summer Olympics with great anticipation. Peter Ueberroth, the chairman of the organizing committee and a savvy businessman, pledged to run the Games without putting the city into debt. That meant the event would rely entirely on corporate donations, sponsorships, and volunteers.

As Chief Medical Director, I was responsible for overseeing health-care services for virtually everyone involved with the Olympics: athletes, spectators, dignitaries, visitors, and support staff. While team physicians were responsible for athletic injuries, everything else, from dehydration and sunstroke to medication management and urgent care, fell under my direction.

Managing hundreds of volunteer physicians, nurses, and medical staff I had never worked with, and who had never worked with one another, was a logistical and human challenge. To make matters more complex, none of them were being paid. Perks like Olympic uniforms and badges were front loaded. Despite signed letters of commitment, there was little real leverage to ensure anyone showed up for their shift, or stayed focused once they did.

I had to strike a careful balance: maintaining enough structure to meet medical needs while allowing space for the excitement and energy of the Games. Staff were qualified and competent, but understandably starstruck. When icons like Michael Jordan, Cheryl Miller, Carl Lewis, or Mary Lou Retton came in for care, everyone wanted to be the one assigned to them. I generally assigned these high-profile cases to the volunteers while I took on the more general cases.

I appreciated that these volunteers were showing up not for a paycheck, but out of a spirit of service and excitement to be part of something historic. I made it a priority to create a positive, respectful environment and to recognize their contributions wherever I could. To the staff's credit, despite the long hours and unpredictable demands, we received very few complaints. Their dedication ensured that we delivered timely, quality care to everyone who needed it, athletes, and spectators alike.

Our family at the LA Coliseum during the 1984 Closing Ceremonies.

Taking on a leadership role where formal authority is limited, like managing volunteers, requires a different skill set. You cannot rely on titles, paychecks, or hierarchy. Instead, you must lead with trust, clarity, and mutual respect. The Olympics taught me that people will rise to the occasion when they feel appreciated, included, and inspired by a shared mission. I was formally recognized for my work and rewarded with premium tickets for my family at the Closing Ceremonies.

Receiving Staff Award after Olympics.

Here are three questions to reflect on your own leadership in similar situations:

- How do you lead when you cannot rely on authority or compensation? Think about a time you had to motivate a team without formal power, what worked, and what didn't?

- What do you do to recognize and appreciate others, especially when their efforts are voluntary or behind the scenes? Recognition does not always have to be public or elaborate, sometimes it is just being present and saying thank you.

- How do you balance team morale with performance under pressure? What strategies have you used to help people stay motivated, especially when the stakes are high or the resources are limited?

Parenting Lessons for Management

Family dynamics taught me much about management, about setting clear parameters for right and wrong, applying rewards and penalties, showing genuine care, and being consistent. My parents were the ultimate bosses, and I saw firsthand how my sisters and I reacted to their behavior.

Growing up, I was constantly on edge, never knowing what to expect. Punishment could come without reason, for imagined misdeeds or for triggering an emotion. At fourteen, already overwhelmed by learning English, keeping up with school, caring for three babies, and handling back-office work for my father's practice, I sat down to dinner one night only to have my rice bowl knocked from my hands by my father, calling me a "Fan Tun" or "rice bucket", only good for consuming rice. He then berated me as a parasite, accusing me of living off his earnings instead of contributing to the family. On another morning, my mother accused me of stealing $20 from her purse. My sisters added fuel to the fire claiming to have seen me take it. Even after the money was found, there was no apology, I was punished anyway.

These experiences etched a lasting lesson: clarity and consistency matter. Rules must be applied based on reason, not emotion. Looking back, I see countless parallels between management and parenting, the setting of policies, the enforcing of boundaries, the power to grant rewards or impose penalties.

THE GOLDEN RULE

For me, management is ultimately about relationships. Since every person is different, there is no single formula that works in every situation. What remains constant, however, is the need for self-awareness. Before managing others, we need to examine our own biases and make a conscious effort to keep them in check. Over time, with experience, we become better at understanding what motivates others, and how to respond in a way that brings out their best.

A simple but powerful principle that guides me is the Golden Rule: I treat my employees the way I would want to be treated. I would want a manager who supports me, who gives me the tools to succeed, and who advocates for my growth. I would want to know that my manager has my back, and that my efforts are seen and appreciated. When I approach leadership from that mindset, I create the kind of environment I would want to be part of.

Keeping this perspective helps me stay grounded. It reminds me that leadership is not about control or superiority. It is about trust, respect, and helping people grow into their potential.

Relationships are two-way streets. You cannot expect loyalty, commitment, or extra effort from others unless you are willing to offer the same in return. This principle becomes especially important during times of uncertainty or crisis, when people are looking for reassurance and leadership.

At Security Pacific, I was managing a team of 200 employees when news broke of the merger with Bank of America. The announcement had been kept entirely confidential, and most of the staff learned about it the same way the rest of the world did, through the morning news. When I arrived at the office that day, the entire 7th floor was in a state of shock. People were gathered in small groups, talking in hushed voices. No one was working. And I could not blame them.

The truth was, most of them would lose their jobs in the coming two years, even though the workload would increase during the transition. As their leader, it was my responsibility to keep operations running smoothly. But how could I expect people to stay motivated when they felt ignored, discarded, and insecure?

I asked myself how I would want to be treated in that situation. With the support of my boss, I created commitment letters and retention bonuses for key managers. These were not grand gestures. The financial cost to the Bank was negligible, since these staff members were needed regardless. But symbolically, it made all the difference.

The commitment letter offered something many people needed most in that moment: acknowledgment. It let them know the company saw them, needed them, and valued their continued contributions. Overnight, the atmosphere shifted. People went back to work with renewed focus. The workload had not changed, nor had the outcome, but that simple gesture of respect restored morale and trust. It reminded me that small, thoughtful actions can have a profound impact, especially when the future feels uncertain.

When people feel overlooked or expendable, motivation plummets. What this experience taught me is that acknowledgment doesn't have to be expensive or elaborate. A simple act of recognition can restore trust and inspire people to keep showing up, even in the hardest seasons.

REFLECTION EXERCISE: LEADERSHIP IN TIMES OF CHANGE

- Think of a time when your team faced uncertainty. How did you communicate with them? What actions, if any, did you take to acknowledge their concerns?

- What would you have wanted from leadership if you were in their shoes? Consider things like clarity, honesty, reassurance, or tangible recognition.

- Write down one small action you can take this week to show appreciation for someone on your team. It might be a hand-written note, a public thank you, or a quick check-in to see how they are doing.

Even a small gesture, when offered with sincerity, can make a lasting impression. When you lead with empathy, you earn respect that no title can guarantee.

ADDRESSING MISTAKES

One area I have always been particularly sensitive to is how mistakes are handled. When something goes wrong, it is tempting for a manager to react swiftly or harshly, especially under pressure. But in my experience, nothing productive comes from public criticism. It only breeds embarrassment, resentment, and fear. That kind of reaction does not solve the problem, and it certainly does not prevent future ones.

Instead, I believe every mistake deserves a private, respectful conversation. Begin by listening. Give the employee space to explain what happened, what led to the error, and how they might approach things differently in the future. Address the issue directly, but make sure the goal is growth, not punishment. Criticism is most effective when it is paired with support and a clear path forward.

Just as important, leaders must own the outcomes in their area of responsibility. Passing blame to protect yourself may save you in the moment, but it will cost you the trust of your team. Over time, this leads to a toxic culture where people focus on avoiding blame rather than solving problems. The best teams operate with mutual accountability and psychological safety. That begins with how we, as leaders, respond to mistakes.

Support Front-Line Staff

It is easy to judge after the fact. When the dust has settled and the pressure is off, everyone becomes an expert in how things *should* have gone. But leadership means standing behind your team, especially your front-line staff, when they are in the arena making fast decisions in high-stress situations.

Whether it is a medical emergency, a customer service failure, or a critical business error, those on the front lines are often forced to act quickly, without the benefit of hindsight. They carry the weight of the moment and do their best with the information they have. It is unfair, and frankly unwise, to pick apart their decisions from the comfort of a conference room the next day.

I lived this reality as a junior ENT resident. One night, a child was rushed into the emergency room, struggling to breathe. In an effort to help, the pediatric resident inserted an endotracheal tube that was too small. Instead of improving the airway, it slipped through the vocal cords and completely obstructed breathing. The child was going into arrest. In that split second, I acted: I performed a tracheostomy, opened the airway, removed the tube, and saved the child's life.

The next morning, during rounds, I was met not with support but with a flood of criticism. Many used the opportunity to show off for the legendary Chief, who happened to be present that day. One after another, peers and superiors piled on, saying what I "should have" done, insisting they "would have" managed without the tracheostomy.

But none of them had been there. None had faced that decision in real time. I will never forget how it felt to be criticized so publicly after doing my best in a life-or-death moment.

Thankfully, the Chief spoke up. He reminded the room that I had been the only one there, and what mattered was that I made the call that saved a life. He said I should be commended, not criticized.

That moment has stayed with me. It taught me that when your people step up under pressure, your role is not to tear them down, it is to support them. Even if you might have acted differently, recognize their courage and effort. A team that feels safe making decisions will grow stronger. A team that fears being second-guessed will eventually stop taking initiative.

Supporting your team, especially under pressure, is one of the clearest signs of strong leadership. People remember how they were treated when things went wrong far more than when everything was going smoothly. When a leader stands behind their staff in the heat of the moment, it builds trust, confidence, and loyalty. On the other hand, leaders who tear people down after the fact only create a culture of fear and second-guessing.

Take a few moments to reflect on your own leadership in crisis situations.

REFLECTION EXERCISE:

- Think of a time when someone on your team made a mistake under pressure. How did you respond?

- Have you ever felt second-guessed or unsupported after making a difficult decision? How did that impact your confidence or motivation?

- What is one specific way you can better support your front-line team when they are facing tough or time-sensitive situations?

Leading well does not mean having all the answers. It means being someone your team can count on, especially when the outcome is not clear and the stakes are high.

Considerations In Hiring Your Team

Throughout my career, I have hired staff at every level, building teams from scratch and filling vacancies. The ultimate decision always rests on two critical factors: whether the candidate *can* do the job, and whether they will *fit*.

Credentials and skills can be assessed during screening. What I focus on are concrete accomplishments, both on the résumé and in conversation. Candidates who try to guess "the right answer" often stumble when I ask whether they have ever disagreed or pushed back on a superior's plan or decision, and how they handled it. Many assume I am testing for compliance. In truth, I value those with the confidence to raise thoughtful concerns.

Growing up, my mother would not tolerate disagreement. She rewarded my sisters for flattering her and ostracized anyone who dared to challenge her. Over time, she became increasingly insular, cut off from friends, detached from the world, convinced that she was always right.

Managers can fall into the same trap. It's natural to gravitate toward people like ourselves, similar personalities, viewpoints, and skills, and far more pleasant to hear good news than bad. But surrounding yourself with "yes" people is dangerous. Those who only tell you what you *want* to hear keep you ignorant of what you *need* to know. Shooting the messenger doesn't make bad news disappear, it only allows solvable problems to grow unchecked.

Today, diversity is rightly emphasized in company missions. But true diversity must go deeper than appearances, it must include ideas, viewpoints, and skill sets. "Talking the talk" while expecting conformity of thought misses the point. I once watched a CEO announce a bold diversity initiative, blind to how his own ego held the company back. His senior management team, all men, mirrored him completely in dress and opinion. Meetings became exercises in ego maintenance rather than genuine discussion.

Without dissenting voices, any leadership group becomes an echo chamber. As William Wrigley Jr., founder of the Wrigley Company, said, *"When two men in business always agree, one of them is unnecessary."*

I have learned that I am most effective when I test my ideas with my team, trusting them to challenge my assumptions, point out flaws, or suggest consequences I might have missed. Their pushback has often led to better plans, or, at times, to abandoning a bad idea before wasting resources. These experiences have been invaluable to my growth and success.

During interviews, I look for authenticity and self-awareness. While I expect respect, I am turned off by schmoozy charm.

An effective organization needs members with complementary strengths. No one excels at everything. Knowing your own strengths and weaknesses is essential to building a balanced team. It's easy to overvalue one's own function: tech people often dismiss marketing and sales as fluff; creatives resist operational details; salespeople thrive on the high of closing deals but dread the logistics of delivery. Yet without marketing and sales, even the best technology can fail to reach the market, as Alan Cooper illustrated in *The Inmates Are Running the Asylum.* And without operations to execute, a strategy remains just an idea. Failure to deliver on promises negates every sale.

I personally thrive on the creative side, strategy, new products, marketing, problem-solving. But success ultimately depends on execution. Early in my career, I often worked alone, told simply to "make it happen." I missed details, made mistakes, and spent time cleaning up afterward. Those experiences taught me to appreciate the vital role of operations and the people who master it. I light up when I see that same passion in others, when an operations person's eyes shine as they describe how they made a plan work. I know those are the people who make success possible.

In interviews, I also look for humility and a positive attitude. Confidence is admirable; arrogance and entitlement are not. Questions about benefits or rapid promotion are red flags. When I ask about past experiences, I listen for ownership, learning from mistakes rather than playing the victim or blaming others.

Above all, I look for authenticity and someone comfortable in their own skin.

Considerations When Firing An Employee

Whatever the circumstance, firing someone is one of the most difficult responsibilities a manager can face. Whenever I interview candidates for management roles, I always ask, "Have you ever had to fire anyone?" If the answer is no, it usually signals limited leadership experience, a hesitation to make hard decisions, or possibly just an extraordinary streak of luck. If the answer is yes, I follow up by asking them to describe the situation. Their response reveals a great deal about how they lead.

Over the years, I have had to fire employees, and I will admit, I did not handle the process well in the beginning. My impatience led me to treat it as a straightforward decision. I relied on objective standards to justify the termination and moved quickly, assuming that was sufficient. Looking back, I can say with confidence that I never fired someone who did not deserve it. Still, I underestimated the importance of due process, not just legally, but in terms of morale and team dynamics.

I have learned to appreciate how a termination impacts the broader staff. Firing someone is never an isolated act. Every employee watches how it is handled. They will ask themselves: "Was it fair?" "Could that happen to me?" If the process seems rushed or disrespectful, it undermines trust in leadership. On the flip side, when poor performance goes unaddressed, it sends the message that expectations do not matter, and it lowers the bar for everyone. Over time, that can drag down the entire team.

Ultimately, there is no perfect way to let someone go. Every situation is different. But the best managers know how to balance compassion with accountability. They give people every reasonable chance to improve while also protecting the overall team's culture and performance. Making that call requires both heart and backbone, and the wisdom to know when you have done all you can.

Letting someone go is never easy, but how you handle it reflects your integrity, leadership, and emotional intelligence. A well-managed termination protects the dignity of the individual while preserving the trust of the team. It is a moment that can shape your reputation as a leader. The goal is not just to make the "right" decision, but to carry it out in a way that strengthens the culture you are trying to build.

Take a moment to reflect on your own approach to these high-stakes decisions:

REFLECTION EXERCISE: MANAGING DIFFICULT PERSONNEL DECISIONS

- Have you ever had to let someone go, or been part of that decision-making process? How did you handle it, and what would you do differently now?

- How do you balance compassion for an individual with your responsibility to the broader team? Think of a time when you saw this done well or poorly. What impact did it have?

- What systems or conversations could you put in place to catch performance issues early, before they require termination? Consider how you could create a culture of feedback, support, and accountability.

Use these reflections to strengthen your ability to lead through difficult decisions, because even the hardest calls, when handled with care, can build trust and integrity within your team.

19

Managing Up

WHEN THE BOOK *Managing Your Boss* came out in 2008, it was seen as a revolutionary concept. But the truth is, everyone has a boss, even the CEO, who answers to a board. Over the years, I have learned that managing up is just as critical to career success as managing a team. Here are a few key lessons from my experience.

AGREEMENT ON EXPECTATIONS AND DELIVERABLES

One of the worst positions you can find yourself in is believing you are doing a great job, only to discover, too late, that your boss had entirely different expectations. You may wonder, how does that even happen? But it happens more often than you think, especially in roles where outcomes are not easily measurable.

Sales targets or client retention numbers are straightforward and quantifiable. But in many roles, job descriptions and performance standards can be vague. When I took the position of Corporate Medical Director and First Vice President of Benefits, the formal job description included language like "promoting employee health" and "optimizing cost and quality of care." That all sounded reasonable until the CEO began our meeting by saying, "The fact that I am handing over millions of dollars to a doctor to manage should tell you just how desperate I am. So, let's skip the small talk, here is what you need to do to prove you deserve the job:

- Reduce the cost trend from 23 percent to under 10 percent within 12 months

- No lawsuits or liability costs. Protect Security Pacific from any liability exposure. Competitor First Interstate lost millions to employee lawsuits for not fulfilling its fiduciary responsibility for assuring quality.

- No unions. One of Security Pacific's competitive advantages was that it still had a non-unionized workforce. Cost reduction of employee benefits cannot trigger a unionizing movement.

He told me plainly that I would keep my job if I achieved these three targets, and lose it if I failed. The pressure was real, but at least I knew what success and failure looked like in his eyes. I had clear, measurable goals.

Although senior leadership had signed off on my strategy, their focus was entirely on financial results, and I was left to handle the collateral issues. To meet the cost targets, I had to limit employee access to only contracted doctors and hospitals. I knew this would upset some employees, despite my best efforts to communicate and manage the transition smoothly.

My instincts told me it was important to get ahead of the narrative. I requested a meeting with the CEO to let him know he might receive hundreds of employee complaints or letters, some potentially even going to the Board. He dismissed my concern and told me he only cared about the financial results.

In the end, he received only a handful of complaint letters, far fewer than he was told to expect, and was more than satisfied with the outcome. I firmly believe that if I had not warned him ahead of time, he would have been blindsided and viewed even a few complaints as a failure on my part. Setting his expectations early helped me exceed them.

If your boss is not clear about your priorities or how your performance will be evaluated, it is your job to initiate that conversation. I learned to send follow-up memos or emails to confirm verbal conversations and clarify priorities. At several points in my career, I took on responsibilities that went well beyond my original job description. In those moments, documenting expectations was critical.

These conversations are not always easy, but avoiding them is risky. You cannot exceed expectations if you are not sure what they are.

ACTION STEP: CLARIFY AND CONFIRM EXPECTATIONS

Take 15 minutes to reflect on your current role. Ask yourself:

- Do I know exactly how success is defined for me in this role?

- Have I had a direct conversation with my boss about expectations and priorities?

- Have I confirmed those expectations in writing?

If the answer is no to any of the above, draft a short email or outline a conversation. Begin with something like:

"I want to make sure I am fully aligned with your priorities. Could we take 15 minutes to clarify expectations and how you will be measuring success in my role this quarter?"

Then, after the conversation, follow up in writing to confirm what was discussed. Clear communication now prevents confusion and disappointment later.

Do not Bring Problems Without Solutions

In my first job at LA County, I was quick to spot problems. I thought my boss would appreciate my attention to detail and initiative. I was wrong. He told me bluntly that he had enough problems already and did not need more people piling on. If I could solve something, then I should do it. If I needed his help to fix it, I should come to him with a specific ask. His message was clear: my job was to make things work smoothly, not to add to the chaos.

That lesson stuck with me. From then on, I made it a rule: never bring a problem without a solution or at least a recommendation.

There is a related lesson I also learned, avoid being a constant naysayer. Even if you are technically right, being associated with negativity can make others tune you out. If your job involves raising concerns, like medical or legal risks, always try to offer a way forward. At USC, I worked closely with the General Counsel on medical school oversight. We often discussed potential risks, but he was selective about what he brought to senior management. When he did raise an issue, he always brought options to help minimize the risk. I still remember him saying, "I can't be effective if I'm seen as just a roadblock."

People remember who helped move things forward, not who pointed out everything that could go wrong. Wherever possible, aim to be a solution-maker, not just a critic.

Building Trust

Trust is that intangible element at the heart of every meaningful relationship. For me, it has always been about actions, not words.

In professional settings, I kept a clear boundary between work relationships and personal friendships. Some of my closest friends today were once my bosses or direct reports, but those friendships developed after our working relationship ended. While working together, I maintained enough distance to preserve objectivity.

It is important to note that building trust was never a conscious goal, it simply came from consistently doing what I believed was right.

While consulting for USC in the mid-1990s, I was on a $10,000/week retainer with Dennis, the Senior Vice President of Administration. My role was to monitor the Medical School's managed care strategy and assess the level of financial risk to the University.

A couple of months into the engagement, I was approached by Steve, the Dean of the Medical School, and technically my superior due to my academic titles. He asked me to help him with his own managed care strategy and offered a $20,000/week retainer, assuring me that he had already cleared it with Dennis.

I understood the politics. Dennis was not in position to say no to the Dean. The new offer would have tripled my annual retainer to over $1.5 Million, and the Medical School presented better long-term career prospects. I could have rationalized accepting it, arguing that Dennis had approved it and I was still serving the same University.

But I declined immediately. I told the Dean it would be a direct conflict of interest. I could not ethically evaluate a strategy while being a part of it. I also refused his request to refer someone else in exchange for a lucrative referral fee, which would have also compromised my position.

Dennis and I have never discussed this directly, but afterwards, I sensed a deeper trust and warmth in our relationships going forward. Even after our professional relationship ended, we stayed in touch until his passing.

To be effective in leadership, I never focused on being liked. What mattered was being respected and trusted. Both take time to earn and can be lost in an instant. I knew my team was watching not what I said, but what I did, how I handled pressure, whether I followed through, and whether I treated people fairly. Consistency, integrity, and follow-through were the pillars that held up that trust.

In the end, it was never about charm or charisma. It was about showing up, doing what is right, and honoring my work through my actions.

SILENCE IS GOLDEN

At some point in your career, you may find yourself in the boss's "inner circle" with access to sensitive or "inside" information. You might become known as your boss's go-to person or confidante. If that happens, be careful not to fall into the trap of becoming the source others go to for the "scoop." It can be tempting to feel important, to enjoy the momentary popularity that comes from knowing more than others. But the cost is steep. If you betray a confidence, you will lose your boss's trust and your coworkers' respect. Once that trust is gone, it is nearly impossible to get it back.

I knew myself well enough to understand I was vulnerable to this. I did not have friends growing up, and a part of me still longed to be included and liked. I am also naturally talkative. I made it a rule to stick to non-work topics or impersonal issues that were already public knowledge. I disciplined myself to keep sensitive information private.

Do not become part of the gossip crowd. Some people are very skilled at baiting you, speaking as though they know more than they do, just to get you talking. Do not fall into that trap. Cut the conversation short. If others start badmouthing your boss, leave. Do not engage. Even if you say nothing, your presence alone may be noted and misinterpreted. In these moments, it is better to walk away and stay above the drama.

FOLLOW THROUGH ON PROMISES – DO WHAT YOU SAY

Talk is easy. Saying you will do something or offering help feels good in the moment, both for you and the person receiving the promise. But follow-through is where trust is built, or broken.

In any relationship, professional or personal, doing what you say you will do speaks volumes. If you follow through, even on something small, people remember you as reliable and trustworthy. If you drop the ball, even on something minor, it can cast doubt on everything else you say.

This is especially true with your boss. If you volunteer for a task or commit to a deadline, keep it. Even if your boss never mentions it again, your ability to remember and follow through leaves a lasting impression. Reliability builds trust over time, and it is that trust that earns you more responsibility and more opportunity.

MEETING DEADLINES

Throughout my career, consistently meeting deadlines distinguished me and helped build my credibility. Completing an assignment on time is one of the most important ways to gain the trust of your boss or your client. It signals reliability, accountability, and professionalism.

Here are some strategies I learned on the job for successfully managing deadlines:

WHEN YOU FIRST RECEIVE THE ASSIGNMENT AND THE DEADLINE

- Assess the context behind the timeline. What factors are driving it? Is your work part of a larger project with others depending on your portion? Is the deadline flexible or fixed?

- Map out everything needed to complete the assignment.

- Identify critical milestones along the way.

- Budget time for each milestone, working backward from the final deadline.

- Anticipate any shortcuts that may need to be taken and think through the possible consequences.

- Schedule a meeting with your boss to review your timeline and plan.

In The Meeting with Your Boss

- Present your plan and walk through the milestones.

- Set clear expectations about any risks that might arise due to tight timelines and offer potential ways to manage or reduce those risks.

- Be prepared to explain how additional time could improve the final result.

- Let your boss raise the question of deadline flexibility. Do not assume it yourself.

When I was looking to leave my job at the University Student Health Center, I saw an opportunity to propose something new, a University Health Plan that would use the University's benefits dollars to generate referrals for the Medical School's private practice. I made the proposal in March and received verbal support from leadership, but became anxious for formal approval so I could begin the work.

Typically, benefits planning starts in May and takes four to five months. It involves analyzing historical claims data, negotiating with vendors, conducting actuarial analysis, and finalizing benefit design, pricing, and cost-sharing, all of which must be approved by both management and employee groups. Everything must be signed off and ready for the printer by October 1 to prepare materials for open enrollment beginning October 15.

Because this would be the program's first year, it also required building and contracting a provider network from scratch, adding more time to an already complex timeline. Without formal sign-off or authority, I was stuck waiting, unable to begin, watching days slip away and the deadline loom closer. It was a powerful lesson in the importance of timely approvals and the need to align expectations from the very beginning.

With University bureaucracy, I finally got the formal go-ahead the Tuesday after Labor Day, shrinking the lead time from five months to just six weeks. I had a tough decision to make. I could tell the University that it was impossible to pull this off for the current year and hope they would still support the idea in the future. Or, I could seize the opportunity and try to meet the challenge, warning leadership that the rollout might be messy and require clean-up afterward. I chose the latter.

I knew the October 15 deadline was immovable. It had already been negotiated with the Faculty Senate and was non-negotiable. I approached the project by working backwards, laying out a milestone schedule to hit every deadline. Here is an example of how the planning looked:

- January 1: Benefits take effect at point of service
- December 15 to January 1: Load enrollment / benefit data and eligibility claim system
- October 15 to December 15: Open enrollment; employee and faculty meetings to explain and market the plan
- October 14: Brochures distributed
- October 13: Brochures returned from printer

- October 9: Review printer's proof
- October 6: Files due to the printer
- September 25 to October 5: Approvals from Faculty Senate (two meetings) and Staff Assembly
- September 22 to 25: Decision and sign-off from Senior Vice President, Administration
- September 21: Present benefit options and financials to Senior Management
- September 20: Develop Senior Management presentation
- September 15 to 19: Actuarial analysis and financial projections
- September 5 to 15: Negotiate discounts with network providers
- September 3 to 5: Review claims data to identify a network of doctor groups and hospitals

I met with my boss, the Assistant Vice President of Benefits, that same day to review the schedule and request clerical support. He understood the challenge, offered his support, and then left it up to me to make it happen. Without time to go through HR channels for new staff, I hired two part-time student workers to handle scheduling and clerical duties.

My emergency medicine background proved invaluable. I was used to crisis management. I inventoried all external resources, including benefit consultants, and put everyone on notice regarding the urgency and need for fast turnaround. The one area with any flexibility was printing, so I negotiated a one-week rush job, which gave me an extra week for everything else.

I treated each milestone deadline as immovable. I timed meetings and presentations to align with completion dates, especially for the parts I had the least control over, like Faculty Senate and Senior Management approvals. Most importantly, I set clear expectations with leadership that this timeline would be tight, and the result would likely be imperfect.

I expected plenty of clean-up in January, but I didn't expect calls to start on New Year's Day. I was cooking and watching football when the phone began ringing. Some hospitals and pharmacies had not yet loaded the benefits / eligibility data and activate coverage. In most cases, I could work with the employee or facility to resolve the issue and arrange reimbursement once offices reopened. In one case, neither side would budge, and I had to put the charge on my own credit card to resolve it.

Aside from the initial planning meeting, I periodically sent memos (this was before email) to keep leadership updated on progress. I never burdened them with the chaos behind the scenes. That was my job to handle. Although I was never formally recognized for the achievement, the trust and credibility I gained with leadership across the University helped my career for decades to come.

The reality is that managing up is about understanding your boss's priorities, aligning your work with their goals, and showing that you can be counted on, especially in a pinch. Delivering results, not excuses, is what builds trust.

ACTION STEP:

Think of a project or responsibility you currently have (or recently completed). Take ten minutes to write out a *reverse milestone map*, starting from the final deadline and working backward to identify the steps and timelines needed to succeed. Then ask yourself:

- Are there any milestones that need more time or support?

- Have I clearly communicated expectations or challenges to my boss?

- What proactive updates can I provide that demonstrate accountability and build trust?

REFLECTION EXERCISE:

- When was a time you took ownership of a tight deadline and delivered?

- What did your actions communicate about your reliability?

- What is one thing you could do this week to strengthen your trust with your manager?

20

Managing Across

TO BE SUCCESSFUL, managers must work with many others beyond their direct reports. Internally, that means coordinating efforts with peers and leaders in other departments. Externally, it means building relationships with vendors, clients, and partners.

The basic principle I follow remains the Golden Rule. Without direct authority, relationships become even more important. I have had to learn to manage both my competitive nature and the warlord-style thinking I grew up with, which treated every interaction like a win or lose battle. The truth is, everyone wants to win. If you insist on winning every time, it usually leads to a lose-lose in the long run.

These interactions are rarely one-and-done. You will almost certainly cross paths again. So even if you "win" today, if others walk away feeling taken advantage of, that loss will return to you one way or another. With co-workers, there is always a next time. With vendors, quality might slip. With clients, they may take their business elsewhere. And remember, the world is small. Positions change, people shift companies, and those relationships stay with you.

It wasn't that I calculated all of this at the time. I simply followed my instincts and what felt right.

Co-MANAGERS

In my first management role at LA County, the organizational chart was complex. There were three separate but parallel administrative tracks reporting to the Board of Supervisors, medical, nursing, and administration. Each department had three bosses. As the Medical Director, I had to work alongside the Nursing Director, who oversaw the nursing staff, and the Administrator, who controlled funding and policy. I quickly learned that if I wanted to accomplish anything, I had to collaborate across all three tracks. In many ways, I approached those relationships like I managed up or handled client relations, I achieved my goals by helping others reach theirs. I pitched my ideas in ways that highlighted their benefit to the other departments. I let others share credit or even take it when it helped move the plan forward.

My work to restructure Triage at LA County is a good example of managing across departments to achieve a shared goal. Triage is a high-pressure role, often assigned to the most junior staff, even though it demands critical decision-making under stress. Inexperienced judgment can lead to dangerous delays or, in the worst cases, life-threatening mistakes.

I proposed creating a new position that required a senior, experienced nurse to staff Triage. While I was responsible for ensuring timely quality care, the authority to create the triage role rested with the Nursing Department, and the funding had to be approved by Administration. It took months of lobbying both groups, but the outcome, improved patient care and better service, made it well worth the effort.

Interestingly, the same principle of placing the most experienced person on the front line was applied at a Verizon store. There, the store manager was stationed as the first point of contact. By addressing many issues immediately and directing customers to the right staff member, the store reduced confusion and frustration, resulting in improved customer experience and higher Yelp ratings.

CLIENTS

As I moved forward in my career, I came to deeply appreciate that clients, whether internal or external, are the ones who pay for your work. Some are thoughtful and reasonable, while others can be difficult and demanding. I always begin with the mindset that the client is right, and then work from there. That does not mean I agree with everything, but I focus on listening and de-escalating. Over the years, I trained myself to stay calm. I take deep breaths and resist saying something I will regret. Even if I know the client is wrong or has misunderstood, it is usually better to buy time. I might say, "Let me look into that and get back to you." This diffuses the tension and allows space to gather facts, find a solution, and return with a thoughtful response. The goal is not to win the argument; the goal is to serve the client.

VENDORS

It is a mistake to see vendors as disposable. Vendors who consistently deliver quality work on time are worth their weight in gold. I make sure they know I value them. That does not mean I pay more or compromise standards. But I treat them with respect. I am punctual, I do not keep them waiting and I rarely cancel at the last minute, unless there is a real crisis. If I am not under a deadline, I don't pressure them unnecessarily. I do not create fire drills unless there is a real fire.

At MedImpact, I was responsible for formulary placement and negotiating rebate contracts with pharmaceutical manufacturers. I approached these meetings with my usual negotiation strategy: come prepared with data, avoid ego-driven tactics, and make sure the other party walked away with something they could present as a win to their leadership.

Years later, many of those same Pharma managers, now promoted, hired me as a consultant to support their contracting strategies. They said they valued my professionalism, preparation, and fairness.

At the time, I had no intention of leveraging those relationships in the future. I was simply doing what I believed was the right thing.

Throughout my career, I have been on all sides of these relationships, as a vendor, a client, a manager, and a peer. I have learned that fairness and mutual respect go a long way. Many of the vendors I treated well earlier in my career became clients of mine later in my consulting work. This was never part of a grand strategy. It was simply the result of long-standing, authentic relationships rooted in trust and professionalism.

BRIDGE TO REFLECTION

Working across departments and organizations can be one of the most challenging and rewarding parts of leadership. When you set ego aside and focus on mutual benefit, you build trust that pays dividends long after the immediate task is done.

REFLECTION EXERCISE:

- Think about a time when collaboration across departments or organizations went well. What made it work?

- Have you ever been in a situation where a short-term "win" came at the cost of a long-term relationship? What might you do differently now?

- What are two specific things you can do this month to build stronger relationships with colleagues, clients, or vendors?

RESOLVING CONFLICTS

No matter the relationship, conflict is inevitable. One strategy I have used effectively to diffuse and resolve conflict is to frame the issue from *my* perspective, rather than accusing the other person. Starting with phrases like "Here's how I see it," or "This is how I'm feeling," opens the door to conversation without immediately putting the other person on the defensive. Accusations often trigger a reaction, but no one can argue with how you feel or how something came across to you. They are more likely to listen, understand your concern, and work with you to find common ground.

Whenever possible, I also rely on framing the issue as a misunderstanding or miscommunication. These are neutral terms that allow both parties to move forward without having to assign blame. More often than not, it creates a path to resolution.

NEGOTIATIONS – AIMING FOR WIN-WIN

Over the years, I have learned a great deal about negotiating, from books, from experience, and from simply watching people in action. I learned to read the room. I learned to spot who needed to be "the smartest person at the table" and whose ego was likely to turn the conversation into a power play. I watched brilliant negotiators who could think on their feet, and I watched others who delighted in steamrolling the other side and bragging about it afterward.

To be successful, I had to settle into my own style, one that felt true to who I am. For me, preparation was everything. Before any negotiation, I always gathered my team for a prep meeting. We would divide all the issues into three categories:

- Must-haves: These are non-negotiable. If we cannot get them, we walk away.

- Nice-to-haves: These are important, but we are willing to compromise.

- Back-pocket items: These are not important to us, but might be important to the other side, and we can use them strategically.

We would also assign who on the team would speak to each issue. Having someone else speak gave me the chance to observe the room and read the dynamics. One of my challenges has always been talking too much, something I had to consciously work on. I practiced using silence as a tool, even counting to myself before jumping in. Silence can be powerful. Often, the first person to speak after a silence gives up more than they should.

Maybe it is my cultural background, but I have never felt comfortable embarrassing someone or forcing them into a corner. While I never budged on my must-haves, I always tried to let the other side walk away with something they could feel good about. I believed then, and still believe now, that a good negotiation allows everyone to leave the table with their dignity intact.

Mediating for Win–Win Solutions

One of the greatest challenges in leadership is mediating conflict, finding solutions that both sides can accept. I think of it as problem-solving for a win–win outcome. Often, understanding subtle sensitivities is just as important as addressing the central issue.

When I became Chief Medical Director for the 1984 Olympics, I had not anticipated how much of my role would involve crisis management and public relations. With dignitaries, celebrities, and world-class athletes gathered in one place, egos and politics were inevitable.

One case remains vivid. A senior Egyptian official visited the Olympic Village clinic with a persistent cough. The diagnosis: tuberculosis. In Egyptian culture, the disease carries deep stigma, comparable to a sexually transmitted infection. Yet tuberculosis is highly contagious and, by law, had to be reported to Public Health. When officials informed him that he would need to be quarantined in a certified TB facility, he threatened to pull the entire Egyptian delegation out of the Games.

I was called to intervene. Neither side would budge.

After considerable negotiation, I worked out a compromise both could accept: Public Health agreed to let me take personal responsibility for the official's treatment, and the Egyptian delegation agreed that he would remain quarantined in the penthouse suite of the Westin Hotel, meeting both medical and diplomatic requirements. This required a great deal of finesse. Each side's ego needed a little boosting. I used premium event tickets to help soften the Public Health leadership's stance. I assured the Egyptian delegation that the CMO herself would be providing personal care, and I made sure the Westin hotel manager had tickets as well, to guarantee extraordinary service and attention.

Both conflict resolution and negotiation require patience, emotional awareness, and the discipline to stay focused on long-term outcomes rather than short-term wins. You do not need to have the loudest voice or the strongest argument to be effective, but you do need clarity, consistency, and emotional intelligence.

Interestingly, some of the people I negotiated against early in my career later hired me as a consultant. I never set out to make friends, but by staying fair and respectful, I earned trust that came back around in unexpected ways.

REFLECTION EXERCISE:

- Think of a recent conflict you were involved in. How did you frame your concerns? Is there a way you could have shared your feelings without placing blame?

- Identify your personal negotiation style. Are you a "talker"? A "wait-it-out" type? Do you go in with a plan or tend to wing it?

- Choose an upcoming conversation or negotiation, and sketch out your version of must-haves, nice-to-haves, and back-pocket items. How might this change your preparation or approach?

BEING UNDERESTIMATED

Standing just 5'3", a minority and a woman, I have gotten used to being overlooked in rooms filled with tall white men. In school, I was able to hold my own because everything was based on objective criteria. But once I entered the workplace, especially when it came to job offers or promotions, the standards became much more subjective. And it is not just about getting the position; it is also about being taken seriously once you are in the role.

As frustrating as that has been, I have come to see that being the "token" or underestimated can work in my favor. Early on, I was given management jobs simply because no one else wanted them. Those opportunities became my training ground. I built experience, developed a successful track record, and positioned myself for greater responsibilities. Because expectations were often so low, it was easier to exceed them. Later, companies saw value in my background and profile to align with the changing market or political climate. While those doors may have opened for different agendas, I was determined to walk through them fully prepared. I might have been hired as a token, but I was never going to act like one.

I will never forget a moment that still makes me smile. I was working at Aetna and leading a team visit to one of our regional offices. My team was arriving separately, and I was the first to get there. I introduced myself to the receptionist as part of the team from Corporate, then sat down to wait for the others.

As I waited, the regional manager came out, clearly in a rush, upset at someone calling in sick, spotted me in the waiting room and handed me a set of papers. He asked me to make copies for the meeting, assuming I was part of the support staff. I didn't say anything. I simply turned to the receptionist and asked where the copier was. I made the copies, returned to the lobby, and shortly afterward, my team arrived.

Once we were all led into the conference room and seated, the same manager walked in and handed me the original documents again, asking me to staple and organize them for distribution. Before I could respond, one of my team members, a man, spoke up. "Why don't we start with introductions," he said. "Dr. Chao, would you like to go first?" The look on the regional manager's face was priceless. I thought he might faint. I just smiled, introduced myself, and carried on with the meeting as if nothing unusual had happened.

Later, I learned that the manager nervously asked my male colleague if I was going to report him or make him look bad. My colleague reassured him: "You don't need to worry; she probably thought it was funny." And I did.

Doing a little clerical work did not make me any less of a leader. If anything, by not making a scene, I gained more respect, both from him and from my own team. I know who I am. I didn't need to prove anything by making someone else feel small. Sometimes, dignity speaks loudest through silence and a little humor.

THE POWER OF BEING UNDERESTIMATED

At the time when the Affirmative Action movement was gaining national momentum, I had gained visibility at USC through the success of the Network Plan. When the University formed a cross-campus Affirmative Action Committee that included students, staff, and faculty, I was appointed as Chair. The position had very little power and was mostly symbolic, a token role meant to enhance public image. Some of my friends thought it was insulting, a mere crumb offered after what I had done for the University. But I chose to view it differently. I used the position as an opportunity to learn more about the University's broader dynamics and, in doing so, raised my profile even further. That visibility helped me negotiate a benefit that mattered, free tuition toward my

MBA. That education would later position me to transition successfully into the corporate world.

When I was named Chief Medical Officer for the 1984 Olympics, I was fully qualified and had already proven myself to the organizing committee. Still, I understood the advantages of my profile at that moment. The US Olympic Committee wanted to project an image of diversity and inclusion. My selection helped advance that narrative. The experience gave me once-in-a-lifetime access and built connections that would serve me in the healthcare industry for years to come.

Later, while at Aetna, I was chosen to be the company's official spokesperson, representing the Company in Clinton's proposed health-care reform. The CEO at the time, Ron Compton, was frank with me. He said that, with the political climate, Aetna would be much better represented by a "minority woman doctor" than by a "white male actuary." That opportunity was a turning point in my career. It gave me a front-row seat to the intersection of healthcare, politics, and public policy, expanding my perspective and deepening my expertise.

Being underestimated can be a hidden advantage. Sometimes people walk into negotiations assuming they don't need to bring their A game. Vendors would come into meetings thinking I was an easy target. While I found it insulting, I kept my reactions in check. I would ask a series of questions, calmly and precisely, until they found themselves boxed in. I never humiliated anyone, but I often left the room having secured far more than they intended to offer. In those moments, I capitalized on being underestimated to my advantage. Ironically, as my reputation grew, I lost that leverage.

No one likes being treated like a token. It hurts to know you are being underestimated. But I have learned to recognize those moments for what they sometimes are, opportunities in disguise. When expectations are low, there is more room to impress by exceeding them. When assumptions are made, you have the power to shift them. These roles, even if offered for the wrong reasons, can lead to the right outcomes. You just need to be ready to step into the space and make the most of it.

REFLECTION EXERCISE: REFRAMING THE UNDERDOG MOMENT

Take a few moments to think about a time when you were underestimated, overlooked, or given a role that felt symbolic more than substantive. Maybe it was a job you were overqualified for, an assignment given with low expectations, or a moment where someone made assumptions about your capabilities.

Now reflect on the following questions in your journal or notes:

- What were the circumstances? Who made the assumptions or handed you the opportunity? How did you feel at the time?

- How did you respond? Did you shrink or step forward? Did you act with grace, grit, strategy, or all three?

- What did you gain? Even if the role or task seemed small or unimportant, what experience, relationship, or learning did you carry with you from that moment?

- What would you tell your younger self now about that situation? Write a short paragraph of encouragement or insight to your past self. Let it be honest and generous.

This kind of reframe allows you to reclaim power in moments that may have felt discouraging or minimizing. Over time, these are often the building blocks of both character and career.

ACTION ITEM: IDENTIFY AND LEVERAGE ONE "OVERLOOKED" STRENGTH

Think of one skill, trait, or part of your story that others may have undervalued in the past, and intentionally put it to work this week.

For example:

- If your empathy has been brushed off as "soft," use it to build trust in a conversation that matters.

- If you were once dismissed for being "too quiet," lean into your listening to ask a powerful question in a meeting.

- If someone assumes you couldn't lead, volunteer to take point on a small project, and lead it your way.

The goal is not to prove others wrong, but to validate your own strength by using it with intention. Write down how you felt afterward, did anything shift in your confidence, energy, or how others responded?

Part Six

The Big Picture

21

Values and Reputation

LATER IN MY CAREER, whenever I met someone new, I often heard, "I've heard a lot about you," or, "Your reputation precedes you." With a name like Schumarry, it was hard to be mistaken for someone else. Over more than 20 years of solo consulting, I never created marketing materials or crafted any formal value statements. Most of my career happened well before the age of social media. Still, word got around.

I would usually respond with a half-joking, "Uh oh…" and more often than not, the reply would be something like, "Don't worry, it's all good." Sometimes they would add, "We've heard you're tough but fair," or "You have high standards," or "You tell it like it is and can be trusted." That reputation was not something I set out to build; I just did what I thought was right. I never assumed anyone was watching. But they were.

One of the clearest ways someone's values show up is how they handle money, in big decisions or small moments. If I get the wrong change, I give it back. If something is missing from the bill, I point it out. I make it a point never to take advantage. Paul and I both knew money mattered, but neither of us ever made a career or care decision based on financial gain. Paul's practice struggled at times, but he never compromised his integrity. On numerous occasions, he would see a patient scheduled for unnecessary surgery after evaluating them and telling them they didn't need it. Even when doing that meant losing business and money, he always did what was best for the patient. To this day, people still seek him out, not for a second opinion, but for the truth.

I fell into Consulting because I was not ready to commit to any job. After Aetna, I was ready to be an outsider rather than be part of any bureaucracy. I quickly learned the reality of the Consulting business. I naively thought that the core business of Consulting was expertise devoid of politics. Instead, I learned that the core business in Consulting was selling and inundated with politics. Back-end deals were pervasive where referrals and kick back "commissions" were standard operating procedures. Many projects were merely to advance a political agenda. I also turned down senior consultant positions from two national consulting firms. In the discussion process, I learned more about their business model. My compensation would be less based on my own billable hours but more on selling projects to generate billable hours for underlings who bill at $250 per hour but are paid $20 per hour.

Fortunately, I had been around enough to have relationships and a good reputation. I build an independent consulting practice purely selling my expertise, giving my best effort to support my client's interest. By no means was I infallible, but my mistakes were honest, with no hidden agenda.

I stayed away from back-end deals or referral kickbacks. As my reputation grew, I was approached with offers to endorse projects I didn't believe in, just because my name and credibility would help push them forward. One major pharmaceutical executive signed me to a $350,000 14-week engagement for a marketing project. He knew that based on previous projects, I had a great deal of credibility with the CEO. A couple of weeks in, he asked me to support a proposal at a meeting requesting millions from senior leadership. The assumptions were flawed, but he didn't care. "Three hundred fifty grand just to nod in a meeting isn't bad," he bluntly told me. I quietly terminated the agreement, refunded payments to date, absorbed the expenses, and walked away.

We've all had that moment when someone asks what we think of another person. A single sentence, "Solid"; "Can be Trusted"; or "a Jerk"; "Opportunist"; or "Watch your back" can summarize years of behavior. That kind of word-of-mouth carries more weight than any résumé, website, or personal branding strategy.

And it is not just the big decisions that shape how people see us, the little things matter too. Do you cut corners when you think no one is watching? Do you take small advantages when you can? Or do you do the right thing even when it's inconvenient or goes unnoticed?

In today's world, it is easy to curate a polished image online. Social media has ushered in an era of personal "branding". That may help amplify your presence, but cannot hide who you are. The reputation that sticks is still built through actions, not appearances. If we want to be known as honest, ethical people, our behavior must match. There will be moments that test us. Sometimes staying true to your values will cost you something, a job, a client, a contract. But the alternative is worse. You may think no one sees, but they do. And even if no one else is watching, you are.

Reputation is like trust, it takes years to build, and one bad moment to lose. In the end, your reputation is your most valuable asset. It reflects who you are. Never compromise on that.

22

Incentives Drive Behavior

IN BOTH LIFE AND WORK, the importance of incentives cannot be overstated. At their core, incentives drive decisions and behavior. Like Pavlov's dogs, rewards and penalties condition our actions and shape culture. Understanding incentives is central to understanding the dynamics of any situation, yet it is often obscured beneath words and surface gestures.

My parents often said they wanted their daughters to be close. Yet, growing up, they sowed division by comparing us and pitting us against each other. When I asserted independence, my mother's resentment led her to reward my sisters for undermining me. They soon learned that pleasing her meant turning against me. It reached the point where I could not even trust my medical school correspondence to be sent home, fearing sabotage, I relied solely on my dormitory mailbox. Later, my mother would lament that I wasn't close to my sisters, never recognizing that her own incentives had shaped exactly that outcome.

The same principle applies in organizations. Companies may champion merit-based missions, but when promotions and bonuses hinge on politics or connections, a political culture inevitably takes root. Employees quickly notice what is *truly* rewarded and adjust their behavior accordingly. Whenever there is a gap between stated goals and real actions, look to the incentives.

Through my management roles with financial accountability, I developed a deep appreciation for how incentives are embedded in complex business models across healthcare. Even when the same terms are used, their meanings vary widely depending on the stakeholder's interests.

Take "quality of care," for example. For patients, it means service, accessibility, and hassle-free payment. For insurers, it means controlling unnecessary care and excess claims. For providers, it depends entirely on how they're paid: under fee-for-service, "quality" often translates to more services and higher costs; under capitation, where providers assume financial risk, "quality" means avoiding unnecessary care.

I remember moderating a payer advisory board meeting focused on the launch of a new drug targeting COPD, which included an offer of "free" diagnostic machines for health plans and medical groups. Before any data was even presented, all the medical director attendees declared they were not interested, focusing on increased costs – operations, diagnostics, and the new drug. Simply, it was not worth the cost of differentiating COPD from asthma when both conditions could be treated cheaply with steroids.

It was only the first 30 minutes of an 8-hour meeting and the meeting was going way off track. It seemed useless to even present the carefully prepared data for further discussion. The sponsors looked to me to salvage the situation.

I went off script, pivoted and asked the attendees if they have had a chance to review the newly released Medicare health risk categories for setting premiums the coming year. When I highlighted that COPD confirmed by diagnostic testing carries the highest risk adjustment in Medicare, raising insurance premiums and at-risk medical group payments by thousands of dollars, the shift was dramatic and instantaneous. The focus immediately shifted from costs to increased revenues.

With the incentives aligned, the advisors immediately began suggesting strategies to remove every access barrier.

What began as a contentious meeting quickly transformed into a love fest. Based on that discussion, the manufacturer revised their marketing strategy, and the product launch exceeded all expectations.

In recent years, "value-based healthcare" has become the industry mantra. But again, each stakeholder defines "value" differently. Pharmaceutical companies focus on medical cost offsets and patient satisfaction; insurers define it as reduced claims; providers often see it as new opportunities for revenue. For patients, lower out-of-pocket costs and service are valued more than long-term statistical benefit.

Understanding these incentive structures is essential for developing sound business and marketing strategies. I have seen countless organizations waste time and resources because they accepted words at face value without grasping the financial motivations behind them.

After one of my seminars, a surgeon approached me about his failing free-standing surgery center. He had invested his life savings, achieved excellent outcomes, and operated at half the cost of nearby hospitals. Despite enthusiastic verbal support from insurers and the local hospital, where his childhood friend was the medical director, he could not secure any insurance contracts or referrals. My first question was who was benefiting from the status quo and receiving the business. The answer was the hospital, but he was assured that both the insurer and the hospital were committed to quality outcomes at lower costs. My on-the-spot analysis was that outpatient surgery was bundled with the hospital's inpatient contracts. Carving it out would cut into the hospital's income and potentially increase the insurer's costs for inpatient care.

I advised him to negotiate a partnership with the hospital so they could share in his profits. Otherwise, he would remain shut out no matter how strong his performance metrics were. Six months later, he told me he had sold his center to the hospital and felt betrayed by his friend.

The lesson is clear: self-interest and incentives are always at the center of human behavior and decision-making. Whether in personal life or business, pay attention to the incentives at play, and whether they align with the stated goals. Unless they do, even the best strategies are destined to fail.

23

Sense of Humor

GROWING UP, THERE WAS not much laughter in my life. Everything was serious, every situation felt like win or lose, life or death. I only ever heard my mother laugh while watching *I Love Lucy*. I noticed she seemed lighter afterward, less critical. Over time, as I began to shift toward a more positive outlook, I slowly learned to laugh too. I came to understand that humor has many benefits, it helps you endure hard times, diffuses tension, and leaves a lasting, positive impression. Remembering some of those moments still makes me smile.

Throughout my journey, I often stood apart and was mocked for being different, from one of only two minority women in a medical school class of 130, to the only woman and only minority in my surgical training program, to the only Asian at Aetna. If I had taken offense every time I could have, I wouldn't have made it. A sense of humor was essential to my survival.

In medical school, our nights and weekends were consumed by dissecting cadavers in Gross Anatomy. One morning, I discovered the penis from a male cadaver inside the vagina of my female cadaver. Everyone watched to see how I would react, whether I'd storm off to report it. Instead, I asked, "Did one of you guys leave something here last night?" Laughter broke the tension, and I earned respect.

Later, during ENT training, senior residents joked that I should practice using surgical tools "like chopsticks." On my surgical rotation at San Francisco General, my male superiors told me I was the only one qualified and assigned me to handle the male patient who caught his penis in the zipper. At Aetna, a security guard, never having seen an Asian employee at headquarters, mistook me for a Chinese food delivery person. In each case, humor bridged the gap, turning discomfort into connection and helping me find belonging in new environments.

Humor also became a tool for public speaking. Even in three-inch heels, I could barely see over most podiums. I switched to a lavalier microphone and moved freely across the stage. I often began by testing the mic, "Can you hear me? Good. Now, can you see me?", which always drew a laugh. When delivering difficult news, I would quip, "If anyone in the back can't hear, there may be someone in the front willing to switch seats." Laughter softened the message and opened the room.

At an elite international conference, a world-renowned German economist intimidated anyone who dared to question his theories or analysis. During his presentation, he showed a photo of himself with his Chinese wife. I had a serious question but didn't want to be berated as others had been.

To break the ice, I began by saying, "Professor, I first want to tell you that you and my husband have something in common, you both have impeccable taste and good judgment in choosing Chinese wives." His stern expression broke into a wide smile, and the audience laughed. When I asked my question, he gave it thoughtful consideration, without a trace of hostility.

Humor can also make you memorable. After Bob Dole lost the 1996 presidential election, he was keynote speaker at a major pharmaceutical conference, packed with disappointed donors. During the Q&A, I had a policy question but decided to start with a little humor. "Senator Dole," I said, "I voted for you, but now I regret it." The room went silent.

He looked tense. Then I added, "During the campaign, you said if I didn't vote for you, my taxes would go up. Well, I did vote for you, and my taxes still went up." The room erupted in laughter, including Dole himself. My policy question hardly mattered after that.

Years later, at the airport in Washington, D.C., I saw Senator Dole again. He spotted me, walked across the waiting area to greet me, thanked me for my humor, and handed me his card with his personal number, telling me to call if I ever needed anything.

Humor also became a bridge in my marriage. Paul has been my anchor for fifty-five years, my Rock of Gibraltar, and just as immovable. In the early years, our strong wills often collided, turning minor disagreements into major battles. Gradually, I learned to use humor to diffuse tension. Paul is a sharp critic but slow to admit his own mistakes. When I noticed this pattern, I began telling him about my own errors first, laughing as I did so. "I wanted to save you the trouble of finding one," I would joke. He would laugh too, and I noticed over time he began catching himself more readily.

I have learned that humor, and the ability to laugh at yourself, does more than ease tension. It builds connection, strengthens resilience, and protects your health by releasing stress and negativity.

24

Reinvention At Any Age

DARWIN'S THEORY OF natural selection is often misinterpreted as "survival of the strongest." In reality, survival depends more on adaptability, the ability to adjust to major shifts in the environment. The same holds true in today's business world.

Only ten percent of the original Fortune 500 companies remain on the list today, and more than half of those added since 2000 no longer exist. Market leaders often become blinded by their own success, unable to see shifts in the market, recognize emerging threats, or seize new opportunities.

A classic example is Eastman Kodak. Once a titan of photography and ranked #16 on the Fortune 100, Kodak's downfall began with its own invention. One of its own engineers invented digital photography, yet the company failed to embrace the technology for fear of undermining its film business. Meanwhile, competitors like Fuji, Sony, and Canon surged ahead. Eventually, Kodak was forced to sell off its patents during bankruptcy proceedings. Even now, the company continues to struggle and has recently warned investors it may soon have to close its doors.

The days of working for a single company for decades and retiring with a gold watch are long gone. In today's rapidly changing marketplace, no company or individual can afford to rely solely on past success. Reinvention is essential. It means recognizing change, seizing opportunity, and building resilience through adversity.

In my memoir, I shared the story of my own reinventions, shaped by dramatic life changes starting in childhood. Before the age of 2, I went from a life of privilege to losing everything. At age 10, I left my family, fled my home, and was thrown into unfamiliar cultures where I had to learn new languages just to survive. As a child, I longed for security and stability, but I learned that change would be a constant, and adaptation a necessity.

In the 1960s, medicine was particularly appealing to immigrants because it offered that longed-for stability. With an M.D., you were almost guaranteed steady work and financial security. In 1960, only about 1,100 doctors graduated from medical school each year. Back then, all you had to do was hang a shingle and you would have a successful practice. By 2024, that number has risen to over 20,000. The explosion of doctors, hospitals, and prescription drugs led to a dramatic rise in health care costs and ushered in a new era: managed care. Many physicians were completely unprepared for this shift. Artificial Intelligence and Robotics now have the potential of fundamentally transforming the practice of medicine.

To balance the demands of work and family, I pivoted away from clinical work and into administrative and management roles. To many in the health industry, that seemed absurd. My husband's colleagues joked about it—who gives up the prestige of practicing medicine to "push papers"? Some even questioned my sanity. But those who resisted change, who clung to the old ways, were left behind. As Spencer Johnson described in his book *Who Moved My Cheese?*, they were the mice still waiting for the cheese that was not coming back.

Change is uncomfortable. It forces us out of our routines and asks us to take risks. There are entire industries devoted to helping people navigate change, books, courses, coaches. But for me, reinvention begins with mindset. It is a mental discipline. I associate change with possibility, not loss. Meditation and self-talk helped me shift my perspective. Confidence builds every time you face something new and get through it. Think of reinvention like a workout: with consistent effort, your adaptability muscles get stronger.

Start small. Try new things. Learn new skills. Say yes to unfamiliar experiences. Practice flexibility in everyday situations. That everyday resilience builds resourcefulness, one of the most important traits in today's world of work.

My early experiences, as painful as they were, taught me how to adapt quickly. Reinvention became a natural part of my professional life. And I came to see that every stage of my life, even the ones I thought were detours, helped prepare me for what came next.

Take Miss Chinatown. At the time, I saw it as a distraction from my path to medical school. But the public speaking and PR skills I gained later became vital, when I served as Chief Medical Officer for the Olympics, and again when I was named the national spokesperson for Aetna during the Clinton health care reform era.

When I left academia and applied for a leadership position at Security Pacific Bank, a Fortune 100 company, I didn't expect to get the job. There were more than 70 applicants, many with better credentials. But I stood out because I could connect with people at every level and creatively solve problems quickly. I credit that to the years I spent waitressing to pay for school, learning how to think fast, multitask, and talk to anyone.

Throughout my career, I chose roles that took me into new parts of the health care system: pharmaceuticals, clinical services, insurance financing, health policy, medical devices. I reinvented myself with each move. And each one made me more versatile, more valuable, and more prepared for the next wave of change.

Reinvention is not just about what comes next. It is about integrating what came before, using every experience, every challenge, as a foundation for future growth.

Wherever you are in your life or career, reinvention is not only possible, it is powerful. You can choose to stay relevant, keep growing, and steer yourself toward your next great chapter.

You may not be able to change the wind, but you can always adjust your sails.

25

The Art of The Pivot

WHEN I ACCEPTED MY first administrative position, I saw it as just a job, not the beginning of a new career path. At the time, Emergency Medicine was still an emerging field, and the management structure was largely improvised. I was brought into the Emergency Trauma division because of my general surgery background. The department chief had come from OB-GYN, and the associate director, Dr. Gerald Crary, was formerly the head of Psychiatry. Both were deeply experienced in their clinical specialties and highly skilled in navigating the politics of the County Health System.

I, on the other hand, had no experience in management. I often turned to Dr. Crary for advice. His wisdom and guidance in those early years were invaluable. Many of his insights stayed with me throughout my career, and I share them here in the hope that they may serve you too.

One of the most important lessons I have learned is how to recognize when it is time to move on, and how to do it gracefully and strategically. Maybe you feel like you have outgrown your role. Maybe the organization no longer values your contributions. Or maybe you are ready to pursue something that aligns better with your long-term goals. Whatever the reason, recognizing that it is time to pivot is a major milestone. Congratulations! Now comes the hard part: executing that pivot thoughtfully.

Whether the transition is something you are choosing or something that is being forced upon you, how you move forward determines what comes next. A successful pivot is not about burning bridges or chasing the next flashy opportunity. It is about pausing to assess, realigning with your values, and positioning yourself to grow in the direction that calls to you.

In the sections ahead, I will share the tools and mindsets that helped me not only survive transitions, but turn them into powerful springboards for reinvention.

How NOT To Pivot

First and foremost, never leave in anger or spite. Even when emotions are running high, resist the urge to burn bridges. A dramatic exit might feel satisfying in the moment, but it rarely serves you in the long run.

Whenever possible, do not leave a position until you have another opportunity lined up. The Chinese saying, "Chi Ma, Zhao Ma" *"Ride a horse while looking for another horse,"* holds true, it is always easier to explain your next step when there are no unexplained gaps in your resume. Many people overestimate how quickly they can land a new role, especially without the benefit of a strong reference from a former employer.

How you leave matters. You will not just leave an impression on your boss, you will also leave one on your coworkers, colleagues, and clients. Even if you are striking out on your own, those relationships may be crucial to your future. They could become clients, collaborators, or trusted referrals down the line.

No matter your industry, you will be surprised by how small the world really is. People talk. Reputations follow. And paths cross in ways you cannot always anticipate.

Leave with grace, keep the door open behind you, and remember, how you exit is part of your legacy.

Preparing To Pivot

Begin by reflecting on what this chapter of your career has given you. What skills have you gained? How have you grown? What challenges shaped you into who you are now?

Even if you are leaving a difficult situation, take a moment to honor the experience. There is always something to carry forward, whether it is resilience, perspective, or a new level of clarity about what matters most to you.

Sit with it. Meditate on it. Let yourself feel proud of how far you have come. That energy will stay with you as you move into your next chapter, and it will influence how others perceive your transition. Positivity is magnetic. When you can speak with grounded confidence about what you have learned and where you are headed, it leaves an impression.

Timeless Wisdom From A Mentor

One of Dr. Crary's hobbies was playing the banjo. He often performed in front of audiences, and he used those experiences to share wisdom that stuck with me for life. He once told me that how you leave the stage is just as important as how you play the song. That became his metaphor for knowing when, and how, to leave a job.

"Leave on a High Note." Just like a performer saves the best song for last, what you do in your final days will leave the strongest impression. *No matter your accomplishments, people will remember how you exited.* Make every effort to leave on a high note. Resist the urge to vent, even during an exit interview, and never badmouth anyone after you have left. Taking the high road always sets you apart.

"Leave Them Asking for One More Song." Dr. Crary said this often when he talked about performance, and I came to believe it applies to careers too. Leave the stage while the audience is asking for one more encore. Likewise, *leave the job when you will be missed.* Do not wait until you are being nudged aside. Your legacy is strongest when others still want you in the room.

...

Of course, there are often triggering events that make us want to leave. The challenge is to not let that moment define how we go. Make every effort to leave on a high note.

...

At LA County, my turning point came after a resident propositioned me as a quid pro quo for his faculty review and my boss brushed it off with "Boys will be boys." I knew pushing the issue could have been counterproductive, so I quietly made a plan to leave on my own terms. As difficult as it was, I weathered the gossip storm set off by the resident's boasting lies. I waited six months until I found a role that would allow me to better balance my career and young family. During that time, I worked harder than ever, ending my tenure on a high note, including designing the new trauma system for Los Angeles and established the LA County Hyperbaric Program, securing Jeff Sipsey as its permanent Director. I gave my boss a full two months' notice, citing family priorities. To this day, I don't think anyone connected my departure with the harassment incident.

...

At Aetna, I was caught in a political storm I didn't fully see coming. I was new, and when I signed off on an expense pushed forward by a business manager who was quietly protecting relatives at risk of termination, I found myself in a policy violation that could have ended my career. After a formal investigation, I was offered reinstatement. For me, it was time to leave. I felt betrayed and resentful of how badly I was treated after giving so much. Even in the terrible days of my father's death, I never missed one political meeting or media interview in support of the Company's agenda. I was also instrumental for Aetna to obtain an insurance license in China by facilitating the application personally with Paul's uncle who at the time, was Chief, Ministry of Insurance for China. But at that moment, I realized that none of that mattered. I worked hard to swallow the resentment and was determined to make my exit a positive one.

I gave two weeks' notice and worked long hours to complete the managed care HR needs assignment. When I submitted that report on my last day, I was met with surprise. Under the circumstances, no one expected it. When I was asked why I bothered, I answered that "A report so important for there to be such efforts to sabotage it needed to be completed". My decision to show up fully in those last days left a lasting impression. I was proud that even in disappointment, I chose to exit with integrity.

...

When I realized that the doors for advancement for me at USC were closed, I made a two-year plan to leave to complete my MBA and achieve tenure for benefits and I worked hard to exceed targets for the Network Plan. When it was time to leave, I gave 3 months' notice to get the University past open enrollment, implementation of the new Benefits year, and solidify Network Plan's foundation for long-term sustainability. 35 years later, that Plan continues to be integral to both USC's employee benefits and its Medical School's private practice. Even though I never expected to cross that bridge again as I ended up doing years later, it was important to me at the time not to burn any bridges at the University.

···

Employees heard the announcement of the "merger" of Security Pacific with Bank of America at the same time as the public, on the morning news. At the same time, the identity of the 5 senior management team members was announced, with the CEO from Bank of America, making it look more like an acquisition of Security Pacific. My boss, head of HR and Legal, would be one of the Executive team. Within a week, I had several attractive outside job offers. I chose to stay because I believed leaving then would leave the Company in a real lurch, escalating the turmoil in the Department which needed to function in the transition. It would be 8 months before I was offered a very high-level position, making me the highest paid administrative staff at the newly merged Bank. I knew that my boss wanted to reward me for my past contributions, but I felt I could not bring a similar value to the merging Company to warrant the compensation, thereby putting her in a difficult position to defend me in a politically charged situation. I turned the position down, leaving for Aetna. I gave two-months' notice, finalizing the benefits for the next year, and working with the head of Benefits of Bank of America to facilitate the assimilation. Although I never crossed paths with my boss professionally again, our relationship based on trust and respect continued.

BUILDING BRIDGES FOR THE FUTURE

Every time I left a job; I thought I was closing the door for good. But over and over, those same relationships circled back to play a role in my future success. My consulting career was built on the foundation of those bridges, former colleagues, clients, even competitors, who had seen me work, trusted my reputation, and opened doors.

Mastering the pivot is not just about knowing when to go. It is about going with grace. Preserve your relationships. Carry the lessons forward. And always try to leave the stage with them asking for one more song.

26

Having It All

HAVING IT ALL" BEGAN** as a catchy advertising slogan, but quickly became the rallying cry, and often the burden, of modern women trying to balance a career and family. While the idea is inspiring, it also creates pressure. When we fall short of this mythical ideal, it can feel like failure.

A friend of my daughter, an Ivy-League educated attorney, recently confided that she feels she "wasted 20 years" staying home to raise her children. Now divorced and with an empty nest, she is filled with regret as she looks ahead. On the other hand, I have friends who reached the pinnacle of their careers, only to realize they missed the experience of building a family. Are we all set up to lose no matter what we choose?

When I was applying to medical school in the 1960s, the concept of "having it all" did not exist. Several interviews required me to pledge total commitment to the practice of medicine, including the expectation that I would never marry or have children. It was presented as a binary choice: career or family.

So, is "having it all" possible? Or is it a myth?

I learned the hard way that balancing a career with family is no simple feat. Having grown up in difficult circumstances, I was used to hard work and believed I could handle anything. But the truth is, I often felt like I was falling short on all fronts. No matter how good my nanny was, she was not me. My husband, steeped in traditional Chinese values, was fully focused on building his orthopedic practice. He believed quitting was a character flaw. My parents had invested in me as the daughter who would carry on my father's surgical legacy. Mentors cautioned that stepping away from a prestigious surgical residency might not only cost me my future, but also set back other women trying to follow in my footsteps.

Still, I knew I could not continue the path I was on.

I made the difficult decision to step away from surgery and move into administrative roles, positions that offered more predictable hours so I could be present for my children. As managed care evolved, I found myself uniquely positioned for senior roles, building a track record along the way. Over time, I built a career that spanned nearly every corner of the health care system. I could not have predicted it then, but what felt like a compromise ended up being the foundation of a much more fulfilling career than I could have imagined.

At a business conference years later, a woman stood up during the Q&A session and asked me, "How did you manage to have it all?" My answer was simple: "Lots of luck, a lot of hard work, and realizing that you can have it all—just not all at the same time."

Life is about priorities. And priorities change.

When my children were young, I made a conscious decision to only accept jobs with regular hours. I wanted to be home when they got back from school. I did not travel for work. I only began taking on roles that required travel after they had grown and gone off to school. A few years ago, when my husband suffered two serious health scares, I stepped away from everything to care for him. During that time, I began writing my memoir, what started as a personal legacy project has now become a book heading toward publication. In the process, I have learned a new field and discovered a new chapter.

Over the years, Paul and I have always made traveling a priority, not only for enjoyment, but for the learnings it offered about the world. We consider it an essential part of our children's education, our personal growth and have organized family trips from their childhood to today. Those shared experiences brought us closer and expanded our understanding about various cultures and perspectives.

Great Wall, China.

Acropolis, Greece.

The Pyramids, Egypt.

Taj Mahal, India.

No experience is ever a waste. Looking back, the skills I used to run a household, creativity, flexibility, organization, and problem-solving, are the same ones that helped me shine later in my career. Arranging playdates and carpools? That is logistics and project management. Making dinner with everything timed just right? That is an operations strategy. Being a mother helped shape me as a leader.

My choices will not be everyone's choices, and that is okay. What matters is that they were the right ones for me.

Your path will be different, and your choices will be your own, but if they feel right for you, then they are right. You can always adapt. You can always reinvent. And with today's advances in health care and science, what was once considered "too late" has shifted dramatically. Whether it is having a child, starting a new business, or launching a second act, it is never too late to begin again.

The best may still be ahead. Listen to your inner voice. Trust yourself. And keep going.

REFLECTION EXERCISE: YOUR COMPASS FOR CHANGE

Life rarely unfolds in a straight line. Careers shift. Families grow. Priorities evolve. Throughout it all, the ability to pivot with purpose, reinvent with courage, and act with integrity becomes your greatest asset.

Take some quiet time with the following questions to reflect on your journey — past, present, and what is next.

WHAT ARE YOUR CURRENT PRIORITIES?

- What matters most to you in this season of life?

- Are your daily choices aligned with those priorities?

- If not, what is one small adjustment you can make this week to realign?

How Have Past Pivots Shaped You?

- Recall a time you changed course — voluntarily or not.

- What helped you navigate that transition?

- What strengths did you discover about yourself?

- Was there a time when being underestimated worked in your favor?

- What did that teach you about perception versus value?

Are You Ready To Reinvent?

- What skills, talents, or passions have been underused lately?

- Is there a part of your story you have dismissed as irrelevant that might, in fact, be a powerful asset?

- What does "reinvention" mean for you right now — personally or professionally?

What Do You Want To Be Known For?

- How do people currently describe your reputation? How does that feel to you?

- What are your non-negotiables when it comes to integrity and how you treat others?

- When the next opportunity or challenge arises, how will your reputation help carry you through?

ACTION STEP:

Choose one of your reflections and turn it into a decision. It could be as small as reaching out to an old mentor, dusting off a shelved dream, or saying no to something that no longer aligns with your values. Write it down. Take the first step. Your future self is counting on you.

27

Security and Happiness Come From Within

AS A CHILD, I USED TO fantasize that something, or someone, would rescue me. Like Cinderella, I imagined I would be swept away into a life of security and happiness. But reality, of course, was quite different.

When I first left home, my focus was purely on survival. In medical school, my energy went into earning my degree. After graduation, I kept chasing titles and roles, hoping that one of them would finally make me feel safe, accomplished, and content. What I did not realize at the time was that every struggle, every small step forward, was quietly building something far more powerful: my confidence.

Each time I failed and got back up, I became a little braver, a little more resilient. Eventually, I began to understand that the joy I felt in reaching a goal was not about the rewards or recognition, it was about the process itself. The same was true outside of work. I discovered deep satisfaction whenever I made a positive impact, no matter how small.

I am incredibly grateful to have found a loving life partner in Paul, but even he could not hand me happiness. And while I have been fortunate to enjoy beautiful experiences and meaningful comforts, none of them compare to the inner peace that comes from knowing I have made a positive difference.

Many people equate money with happiness. We often hear things like, "I'd be happy if I made X amount," or "I'd be happy if I could buy my dream house or afford certain luxuries." But can money truly buy happiness? In my view, money contributes to happiness not through the things it can purchase, but through the freedom it provides — the freedom to make life and work choices without constant financial worry.

Over our fifty-five years together, Paul and I have experienced both lean times and years of unexpected windfalls. Regardless of our income, we have always maintained a mindset of prosperity, never feeling or acting truly poor or particularly rich. Our spending habits have remained steady. I have never minded shopping at Costco, thrift stores, or Dollar Stores, and Paul still takes pride in his $10 haircuts and his Toyota.

When our children were growing up, we prioritized their education above all else. We paid full tuition for private schools and top-tier universities so they could graduate debt-free.

Stephen, Andover graduation.

Lisa, Stanford graduation.

Stephen, CMU graduation.

Lisa, Columbia Law graduation.

We have always lived by the principle of "living below our means," and we never let money dictate our professional decisions. Paul's medical practice was solely focused on what was best for the patient, not on the financial incentives. Despite taking an 35% pay cut, I turned down Bank of America to go to Aetna and learned about the insurance industry, health policy and corporate dynamics. Despite taking an 80% pay cut, I left my consulting practice to be part of the start-up team at MedImpact and learn a whole new aspect of health care, pharmaceuticals. These learnings s expanded my expertise and enhanced my value exponentially later in my career. Today, Paul and I are grateful to be able to indulge in experiences and things we enjoy, but more than anything, it is the peace of mind from not having to worry about money that feels like the greatest luxury of all.

There are countless books and articles written about the pursuit of happiness, but I believe the answer is much simpler, and closer, than we think. For me, happiness is found in gratitude for what I have, and in continuing to offer something good to the world around me.

And the best part? That kind of happiness is fully within our own control.

Part Seven

Reflections

Connecting The Dots Looking Backwards

WHEN MY DAUGHTER Lisa graduated from Stanford, it was a few years before Steve Jobs delivered his now-famous commencement address there. Although I was not there to hear it in person, I have watched it online many times since. It remains the only commencement speech he ever gave, and in my opinion, it is the best one ever delivered.

In it, Jobs shares three life lessons. The one that struck me most was this: *You can only connect the dots looking backward, you cannot connect them looking forward and plot your path.* No one can predict the future. The pace of change is accelerating and it is up to each of us to read both the organizational and market signs to pivot with the changes. Jobs tells the story of taking a calligraphy class simply because he loved it. At the time, it seemed completely impractical. But years later, that very class became the foundation for all the fonts used on computers today. He could not have known then how that random interest would shape the future of technology.

His insight deeply resonates with me. I could never have predicted that a baby born in Mukden to a warlord family, or a little girl raised in Beijing during wartime, would one day find herself living a full and rewarding life in the United States. Early in my life, I did whatever I could to survive. As painful as many of those struggles were, they became foundational lessons that taught me resilience, adaptability, and resourcefulness.

Who would have guessed that the skills I developed during those hard times would help me land my first major role at Security Pacific? Or that a spontaneous decision to do a medical externship in Hawaii would lead me to my life partner? I did not plan my career in a neat arc. I made decisions based on what felt right in the moment and what I hoped to learn next.

At the time, I was devastated not to receive a promotion I wanted badly at USC. But in hindsight, staying might have limited me. That disappointment opened the door to opportunities in the outside world I never could have imagined. What once felt like failure, I now see as redirection.

I could never have charted this path with its detours in advance. Yet each of those dots, each moment of struggle, choice, risk, or leap of faith, has become a point on the map of a phenomenal journey. They all connect. And they all brought me here.

Chao Sisters with Family Christmas 2025.

REFLECTION EXERCISE: MAPPING YOUR OWN DOTS

Take a moment to look back, not to dwell, but to discover. The path may not have always made sense at the time, but what connections can you see now?

- What past experience felt frustrating or disappointing at the time, but now reveals itself as a turning point? What did it lead to that you couldn't have foreseen?

- Think of a "random" skill, job, or encounter you once dismissed. How has it shown up again in your life in a meaningful way?

- What is a dot you are placing now—something uncertain, risky, or new? Even if you cannot see the outcome yet, how can you trust that this moment has value?

Let your answers guide your perspective. You do not need the whole map to take the next step. Just trust that one day, it will all connect.

The Journey and The Truth

AS I LOOK BACK OVER my life, from the chaos of childhood to the long arc of my career, I see that nothing was wasted. Every hardship, every detour, every triumph, and every disappointment offered me something: a skill, a strength, a deeper understanding, or a necessary awakening. Each experience, whether painful or triumphant, became one more thread woven into the silk purse of my life.

There were times I thought I was failing. At times I thought I was stuck. At times I thought I was alone. But with time, distance, and grace, I have come to see that I was always becoming stronger, more self-assured, more grounded in who I really am. And if there is one truth I can offer you, it's this: you are not stuck, you are not late, and it is never too early or too late to grow into who you were meant to be. Every thread has its purpose.

I wrote this book not to teach, but to share. My story is just one story, but I hope it reminds you of your own power to face the hard things, to make brave choices, and to trust the quiet knowing inside yourself that always points the way forward.

You do not need to have it all figured out. You only need to keep showing up, to your values, to your voice, to your life, with as much honesty and hope as you can. That is success. That is leadership. That is enough.

And if you forget, come back to these pages. Come back to your notes, your memories, and your wisdom. You already have every thread you need to weave your own silk purse, your own version of a life shaped by purpose, courage, and abundance.

This is not the end. It is simply the next beginning.

Schumarry H. Chao, MD, MBA

www.schumarrychao.com

Schumarry Chao is a distinguished healthcare professional whose career spans emergency medicine, academia, managed care leadership, and strategic consulting. A board-certified emergency medicine physician, she holds multiple degrees from the University of Southern California and University of California, San Francisco. She has built a career at the intersection of clinical excellence, operational strategy, and industry innovation.

Dr. Chao has served in several high-impact leadership roles, including Chief Medical Officer for the 1984 Summer Olympics, where she oversaw large-scale medical operations for an international audience; Director of Emergency Trauma, Los Angeles County; Director of Health Benefits, University of Southern California; 1st VP and Corporate Medical Director, Security Pacific Bank; VP and Corporate Medical Director, Aetna; and Chief Medical Officer for MedImpact Healthcare Systems, where she helped grow membership from 200,000 to 28 million lives. For 10 years, he served on the Board of Trustees, University of Sciences, Philadelphia. She later founded SHC & Associates, a consulting firm focused on healthcare strategy, value-based care, and cross-stakeholder alignment.

A Clinical Professor at the University of Southern California, Dr. Chao is widely known for her ability to bridge clinical medicine, public policy, economics, and the evolving needs of the healthcare market.

Key Contributions and Areas of Expertise

Healthcare Strategy

Dr. Chao is known for her strategic and operational leadership across every major sector of the healthcare ecosystem—including health plans, delivery systems, employers, and the pharmaceutical industry.

Value-Based Care

She is a noted expert on shifting healthcare's focus from cost control to value creation, with published work such as:

- *Shifting the Focus From Cost to Value: Key Stakeholder Perspectives*, Journal of Managed Care & Specialty Pharmacy (Chao SH, Edgar B., 2006). https://www.jmcp.org/doi/abs/jmcp.2006.12.S6-B.1

Health Policy & Innovation

Dr. Chao's scholarship includes contributions to federal policy discussions and large-scale health improvement initiatives:

- *Medicare Section 1013 and AHRQ's Effective Health Care Program*, National Institutes of Health (NIH) (Chao SH, Urbano FL., 2007). https://pmc.ncbi.nlm.nih.gov/articles/PMC10437467

She also participated in high-profile national panels such as the Workforce-Health-and-Productivity Summit, contributing alongside leaders including Cathy Baase, Nancy Desmond, Dee Edington, and John Howard.

Industry Visibility & Commentary

Dr. Chao has been featured as a leading healthcare strategist and analyst in major media outlets, including multiple *Los Angeles Times* reports:

- *Health Industry Prognosis Looks Good to Wall Street* (2000).
- *Pressures Force HMOs to Evolve or Succumb* (1998).

Pharmacy & Managed Care Leadership

Her work in pharmacy benefit strategy and mass customization has been influential in the managed care space, including:

- *Mass Customization: The Next Generation of Pharmacy Management*, AJMC®, 2003.
- *The HIV Landscape in a Managed Care Environment: Current Challenges and Potential Solutions*, JMCP, Chao SH.

Cost-Effectiveness & Productivity Research

Dr. Chao contributed to foundational research on integrating cost-effectiveness into policy decisions:

- *Strategic Plan for Integrating Cost-Effectiveness Analysis into Health Policy Decisions*, NIH, Neumann PJ, Chao SH, et al., 2008. And studies examining the impact of health conditions on workplace productivity (Chao SH., 2025).

Professional Identity

Across her career, Dr. Chao has built a reputation for:

- Bridging clinical and business domains with clarity and rigor

- Navigating complex political and operational landscapes

- Introducing innovative benefit strategies and value-based frameworks

- Translating data and evidence into actionable solutions

- Advising organizations on stakeholder-aligned healthcare strategy

Her work has shaped benefit design, managed care innovation, and policy dialogue for more than three decades.